Contemporary Knitting
for Textile Artists

Ruth Lee

Contemporary Knitting
for Textile Artists

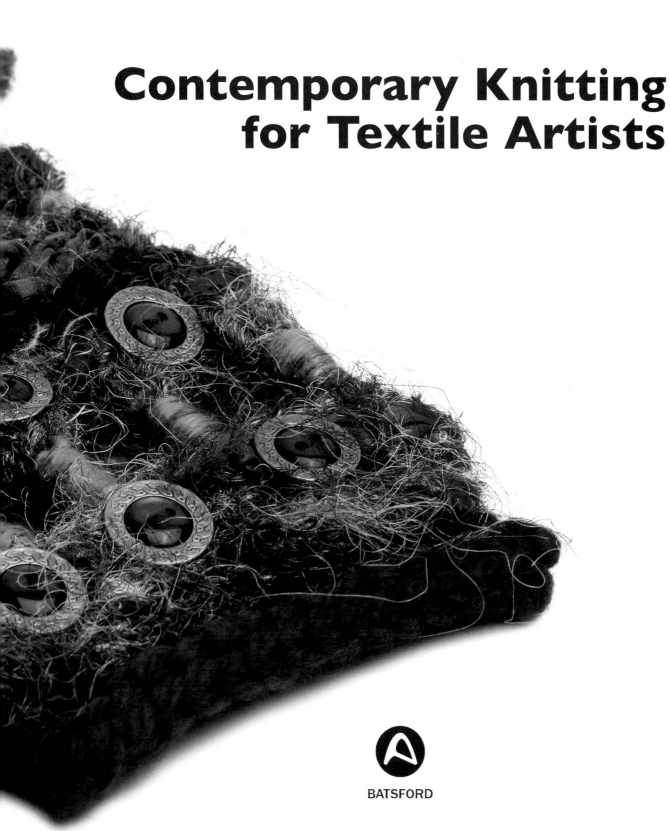

BATSFORD

Remembering my mum Marjorie whose support and encouragement made all this possible and to my partner Mick Pearce for living through the challenge of yet another deadline: your sense of perspective is invaluable.

Thanking John Allen for his timely support and encouragement to push my own personal boundaries for which I am ever grateful. Thank you.

First published in the United Kingdom in 2007 by
Batsford
10 Southcombe Street
London W14 0RA

An imprint of Anova Books Company Ltd

ISBN-13 9780713490466

A CIP catalogue record for this book is available from the British Library.

15 14 13 12 11 10 09 08 07
10 9 8 7 6 5 4 3 2 1

Reproduction by Anorax Imaging Ltd, England
Printed by Craft Print International Ltd, Singapore

This book can be ordered direct from the publisher at the website:
www.anovabooks.com, or try your local bookshop

Distributed in the United States and Canada by Sterling Publishing Co.,
387 Park Avenue South, New York, NY 10016, USA

Contents

Introduction

With the current revival in hand knitting gathering momentum many people have become interested in using traditional two- and three-dimensional knitting in new and innovative ways, as a method of communicating ideas rather than simply as technique for its own sake. This book sets knitting in a modern context for the contemporary fibre artist, craft maker, textiles student and enthusiast. Use it as an inspirational resource to help you to develop your own practice further, for example by moving into outdoor installation work, gallery pieces, wearable art and body adornment.

Throughout the book I place emphasis on the relationship between actual making and the visual language of art and design. Experimental surfaces and structures are sampled in a range of naturally occurring and synthetic materials, such as wire, paper yarn, plant materials and plastics, found and recycled materials, rope and elastics. Instructions on producing these samples are accompanied by in-depth information on technique, and the individual properties of fibres and other materials, giving you a sound understanding of all aspects of the processes involved. By 'thinking with your hands' you will be exploring the connection between these different facets of knitting, and simultaneously unlocking your creativity. You do not need to have a traditional art and design background – contemporary knitting is about original thinking and a sensitive handling of technique, materials and concepts.

Knitting is not an esoteric mystery. It is a logical process whereby knit stitches, purl stitches, or a combination of knit and purl stitches, form one unit of pattern that then builds through repetition into simple or complex structures. There is no mystery to the stitches: a purl stitch is simply a knit stitch in reverse, with the ridge or knot of the purl stitch facing towards the knitter, rather than away. Stitches can be knitted two together, increased or decreased, worked into more than once, slipped or cast on or off in any number of configurations. Whatever you are doing to the stitch, it will always be worked with the yarn at the back of the knitting (for knit stitches) or with the yarn at the front of the knitting (for purl stitches). Knit and purl stitches are the building blocks for all the different stitch patterns in knitting, from rib patterns, cables, lace, textured patterns and colourful jacquards to stocking stitch, garter stitch and free-form knitting.

Fundamentally, knitting is all about the relationship between stitches, gauge (tension), knitting medium and finished fabric. In this book, knitting surfaces and three-dimensional forms are simply seen as an extension of this relationship, which is similar to the way a drawing is constructed from a series of lines and marks in various media on a chosen drawing surface. Yarns and fibres substitute for drawing's pen, pencil or charcoal, while stitch structures compare to making a mark on a surface. Indeed, one might think of knitting sample patches as a way of making thumbnail sketches and drawings – only, in this case, with knitting needles and yarn.

above

Nymph, knitted in single-core connecting cable.

Using this Book

This book assumes a basic knowledge of knitting, with more attention given to a creative interpretation of technique rather than basic knitting know-how. However, my initial aim is to return you to these basics, so that you can build a strong foundation from which to launch your own experimental knitting. Understanding exactly what you are doing, at a fundamental level, will give you the ability to devise your own stitch patterns, unpick mistakes with confidence and, eventually, deconstruct existing stitch patterns. Seeing beyond the superficial decoration and reducing a pattern down to its underlying structure gives you a point of departure for your own patterns and designs.

The shorthand jargon of knitting patterns can be off-putting to the beginner, just as a music score is incomprehensible to someone who lacks knowledge of the rudiments of music theory. Both reading knitting patterns with confidence and constructing a piece of knitting from scratch require a basic knowledge of stitch structure, which is why pattern information is written out in longhand here. Once understood, it is easy enough to translate it into the more widely used knitting shorthand.

Ideally, learn to develop patterns from scratch, just as you learned to write letters of the alphabet, words and – finally – joined-up text, rather than following existing knitting patterns on automatic pilot. Abandoning commercially produced stitch pattern guides lets you take personal control of your knitting experiments, but can be daunting. With this in mind, I have included some confidence-building exercises that will help you to make the leap.

The sampling examples throughout the book provide a way of understanding how a particular technique works, but you should feel free to move on to your own ideas. The emphasis is on constructing the textiles rather than focusing on finished projects, so the samples throughout will suggest any number of applications, whether purely functional or as a fibre-arts statement. I encourage you to explore hands-on experimentation and to hone your craft skills through practice, so that they become second nature and you can go on to translate your own creative ideas into something tangible and original.

Starting from an overview of necessary and useful equipment (most of which is cheap, portable and quiet to operate) the book then surveys the different materials available to the adventurous knitter, and discusses their properties. Subsequent chapters cover different working methods that you can develop further as single techniques, or combine. An overview of each technique is given with one or more working methods outlined in detail with supporting samples. Space does not permit an in-depth discussion of every variation of all of the techniques sampled. Similarly, the nature of this book means that some topics had to be excluded. For example, any discussion of English, Continental, Eastern and combined working methods was omitted, as is detailed information on needle and hand positions, and the way the yarn is tensioned. There are many excellent books and web sites available, and a suppliers list for all the commercially produced yarns and fibres used in the book is also included (see page 124).

Finally, a word on hand and machine knitting. In my own practice, I regard both as simply a means to an end, with my choice determined by my chosen technique, the knitting medium and the scale of the work. A knit stitch is the same whether it is worked on a machine, on knitting needles or on a frame loom. Many of the ideas in this book can be translated to machine knitting with even an elementary knowledge of the domestic knitting machine.

Choosing the Right Tools

Needles

Needles are an essential piece of equipment for your knitting, be they single-pointed, double-pointed or circular. They come in a wide range of materials: for example, steel, nickel plated, aluminium, metal alloys, various woods, plastics, resin and bamboo. Each type of needle has its own particular merits and will handle differently, so experiment with various types and sizes of needle in relation to the materials you are knitting.

Needles sizes range from 0.5mm (US size 8-0) fine-steel needles, intended for lace knitting and working in miniature, to wooden broomhandle-size needles. Single-pointed needles, which are straight with a stop at the end, are manufactured in pairs. Double-pointed needles, traditionally used for working in the round, are sold in sets of four or five, while twin pins (circular knitting needles) have points at both ends, and can be used to make straight or tubular knitted fabrics.

When it comes to material, needles manufactured in reinforced plastic or resin are a relatively inexpensive option, allowing the novice knitter to build up a good collection of needles in various sizes and lengths. Lightweight and durable, they are useful for knitting many of the textured modern yarns and also many of the more unusual materials suggested in this book (with the exception of some plastic materials). A good selection of these needles is available from Pony in a wide range of sizes up to 25mm (US size 50). Their slightly blunt points, compared with steel needles, are especially useful for knitting loosely spun yarns and handmade 'yarns' – made from knitted tubes, crochet chains, paper yarns and rough-cut fabrics, for example.

Lightweight bamboo and birch wood needles are warm to the touch, and less tiring on the hands than metal or plastic. Both types of wood have an inherent strength and do not warp easily. Ideally, look for needles made from wood sourced from regulated forests, such as those made by Brittany Birch Knitting Needles. Double-pointed needles, as well as straight and circular twin pins, are available in various types of wood.

Wooden needles have the advantage that stitches are less likely to slip off, particularly when working with slippery hair fibres such as mohair and alpaca, or Rowan Big Wool and Colinette Tao 100 per cent silk. The same applies to smooth tape yarns, such as paper yarns, soft cottons and eco yarns such as bamboo and corn fibre yarn. Light plastic materials, such as bubble wrap and cling film (Saran wrap), for example, are also easier to knit on big wooden, rather than plastic, needles. Of particular interest are the square-section needles marketed by Kollage,

opposite

Straight needles in aluminum, palm wood (square cut) and birch.

handmade in Vietnam from Forest palm. These are claimed to be easier on the hands than traditional round needles, and to produce more uniform stitches. They are surprisingly comfortable and lightweight to work with, while the square profile does indeed seem to help to maintain an even tension with smooth flat tape yarns, such as Cornucopia and Amaizing 100 per cent Corn Fibre (hence the name), both available from South West Trading Company (SWTC).

Multi-purpose double-pointed metal needles, 20cm (8in) long, are supplied in sets of four in the Pony brand. Addi manufacture the same length, in plastic, in sets of five, including needle size 20mm (US size 35). The latter are useful for knitting strips of fabric and wide ribbons, as well as doubling up as extra-large cable needles.

Traditional steel needles are strong, with sharp tips, and are useful for the complex increases and decreases found in openwork stitch patterns: for instance, those manufactured by Innox in sets of five, 20cm (8in) in length. Plated steel needles in really small sizes are tempered so that they will not break, while exhibiting a degree of flexibility. Steel and aluminium needles are best for knitting enamelled copper wire, though single-core electrical cabling (for example) works well when knitted on large plastic needles. There is a tendency for wire stitches to slip off metal needles, but they usually keep their shape and are easily picked up. Use a stopper on the end of the needles when not in use.

Sizes differ between Europe and the United States, and older knitting needles are often sized in old English sizes and imperial for example, rather than metric units. For example, 0.5mm is UK size 22 and USA size 00000000 (8-0). Use a needle gauge (available from Addi) or refer to websites that show comparative needle sizes.

The needles shown on the previous page are an assortment of straight knitting needles in aluminium and wood. The top sample, knitted on aluminium Pony needles, is worked in string and the sample below it uses a selection of tape yarns. The brown wooden needles in the centre are made from palm wood and have a square profile with a sample knitted in Cornucopia, a yarn made from maize fibre. The 4mm (US size 6) needles at the bottom, made from birch, show samples in Colinette Tao silk yarn with glass beads.

below

Double-pointed needles. Here you can see some of the ways in which these versatile needles can be used.

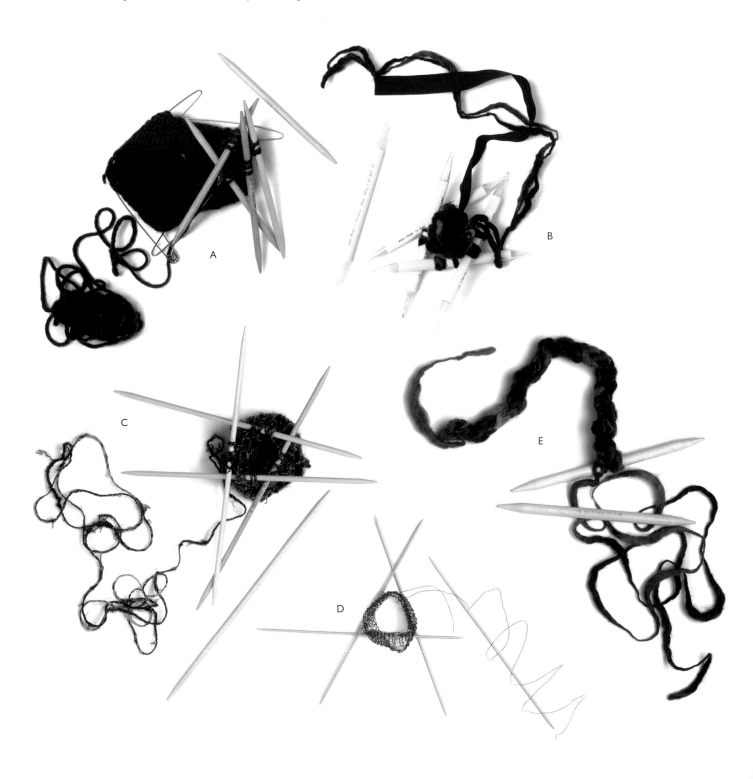

Double-pointed needles are versatile, and can be used in various ways, as shown opposite. Birch needles (A) in a mid size are comfortable to hold. When working a small section, such as the finger of a glove, put the stitches not in use on stitch holders. Plastic needles, like these from Addi (B), are fun to use, here shown working with ribbon and Colinette Point 5. Often you will want to work in the round with four needles holding the stitches plus a fifth, working needle, as in the set with the recycled sari silk yarn (C), but if the piece is very small or you don't have many stitches, you can use three needles plus the working needle as on the sample worked in wire (D), or you might work with just two needles in the traditional way or when making i-cord (E).

The third basic type of needle is the circular needle, like the ones shown below, which are all made by Addi. The sample, bottom right, is worked in South West Trading Company (SWTC) bamboo yarn and Colinette Tao. As the sample expands it can be transferred to a longer needle.

below

A selection of circular needles.

Knitting Frames

The frame below is a round, plastic knitting frame – these are sometimes referred to as knitting looms, knitting boards, spool frames or scarf boards. These are sold in varying dimensions and gauges. The Nifty Knitter is of plastic construction with grooves in the pegs to assist the knitting process. Many frames are adjustable to accommodate different widths of knitting.

When using knitting wire or plastics, spool frames are kinder on the hands than conventional knitting needles. By winding the wire around the pegs, then lifting one stitch over the other with a pick or crochet hook to make the stitches, you can avoid the need to tension the wire around your fingers, which can cause blisters and surface cuts if you are knitting a great deal (see chapter 6 for more on spool and frame techniques).

Frames are easy to make yourself. The simplest way is to make a temporary spool by taping lolly (popsicle) sticks around the edge of a sturdy plastic drinks cup that has the bottom cut off (a roll of cardboard or cardboard tube could serve the same purpose).

below

Circular knitting frame.

Small Tools and Other Equipment

These include therapeutic craft gloves (see below for more on health and safety issues), sewing needles, scissors, wire cutters, tweezers and shallow containers for picking up and storing beads. You will also need small steel crochet hooks, latch tools and rug hooks with latches. Useful equipment includes ball or cone winders, sturdy wooden hank winders for specialist yarns, such as those from Colinette, and a dedicated cord maker.

In addition to a range of art materials and sketchbooks for experimental surface manipulation, consider buying a hot-air blowing tool and soldering iron. Optional larger equipment includes a basic, no-frills knitting machine, a computer (with printer, digital camera and scanner) for visual- and text-based work, a sewing machine and a needle punch/embellishing machine (see the section on needle felting in chapter 9, page 113, for more information).

Health and Safety Issues

It is essential to be aware of health and safety issues, and to use all potentially hazardous materials and equipment responsibly. For example, when burning any type of materials you should take all necessary precautions and be aware of any possibility of poisonous fumes. When using any type of chemical – solvents, glues, varnishes, bleach and dye powders – read and act on the relevant health and safety guidelines for each product.

RSI (repetitive strain injury) is thought to be caused by repetitive movements over a long period of time, and can be a hazard to textile makers. If you think that you may have problems relating to RSI then seek professional advice. Possible avenues to explore included learning to knit by holding the needles and yarns with both left-handed and right-handed tensioning methods, so as to vary your movements. Investigate knitting with circular needles rather than straight pins, and experiment with a range of needle types and weights to determine those that suit you best. Consider wearing therapeutic craft gloves if they will assist you.

Good posture, seating height and lighting are of paramount importance when knitting. If you knit for long hours you should take regular breaks, and exercise your back, neck and hand muscles in particular. If all else fails, set a timer to remind you to stop for breaks every 20 minutes or so.

On a practical level, heavy, large-scale work can also present physical difficulties for the knitter, some of which can be solved by knitting individual sections and only linking them together at the making-up stage (for example, see the bias knitted rug sample on page 33). Alternatively, you can make use of a support, such as a table, to take the weight of the knitting as it progresses. *Spirit Dresses* 3 and 4 (see chapter 10) were made in this way – standing up to knit. When working with very large broomhandle-size needles try knitting with the needles balanced on the floor, and knit back and forth without turning the work.

Essential Knitting Know-How

Anatomy of Knit and Purl

You might like to refresh your knowledge of the fundamentals of knitting before moving on to more experimental work. Understanding how the two basic stitches are formed allows you to analyse existing examples and, importantly, provides the building blocks to create your own designs from scratch.

The sample opposite illustrates a range of basic knit and purl stitch patterns in a smooth, easy to knit, commercially produced yarn, using the ball-band guide for suitable needle sizes. The example shown is knitted in Bigga by Sirdar on 15mm (US size 19) plastic knitting needles. Another suitable yarn for this purpose is Big Wool by Rowan.

To make a knit stitch the knot of the stitch faces away from the knitter, whereas a purl stitch has the ridge or knot facing toward the knitter. When working on two needles, and the knitting is turned at the end of each row, you will notice that there are ridges on both sides of the knitting if you work every row as a knit row. This type of stitch structure is known as garter stitch (see section A of the sample opposite).

However, if every other row is a purl row then you will find that the fabric is smooth on one side and textured on the other. In this example all the knots of the stitches are on the same side of the work. You can use either side of the knitting as the 'right side' (see sections B and C).

Combine knit and purl stitches in the same row to create vertical ridges and furrows in the knitting. Conventional 'knit 2, purl 2' rib is made up of unbroken vertical columns that alternate pairs of knit and purl stitches (see section D). To work this type of rib over 12 stitches (or any number of stitches divisible by 4) the second and all subsequent rows are commenced with the opposite stitch to that with which the previous row ended. In this example the row commences with 'knit 2' and ends on 'purl 2'. Turn the work and repeat these instructions throughout. But if you cast on 10 stitches, you will both begin and end the row with two knit stitches. In this case the next and every alternate row will commence and end with two purl stitches (a 'purl 2'). Here, the smooth side of the purl stitches is facing when the work is turned in readiness to knit the next row. Beginning the second row with two knit stitches means that the knot of the knit stitch is on the reverse of the work and the smooth sided is facing.

To knit a broken rib (see section E) work the first row as described above for 12 stitches. Commence the second and subsequent rows with the same stitch as that which ended the previous row. In this example the second row begins with two purl stitches ('purl 2') and ends with two knit stitches. These two rows form the pattern and should be repeated throughout to form the broken rib.

More complex textured patterns involve combinations of knit and purl stitches where, for example, a knit stitch might sit directly above the knit stitch from the previous row, thus creating ridged sections, and vice versa with purl. For example, to knit a diagonal rib (as shown in section F) work the following pattern. Eight rows and eight stitches form the pattern repeat; the pattern unit is centred over the middle eight stitches (see graph on page 17) and the four

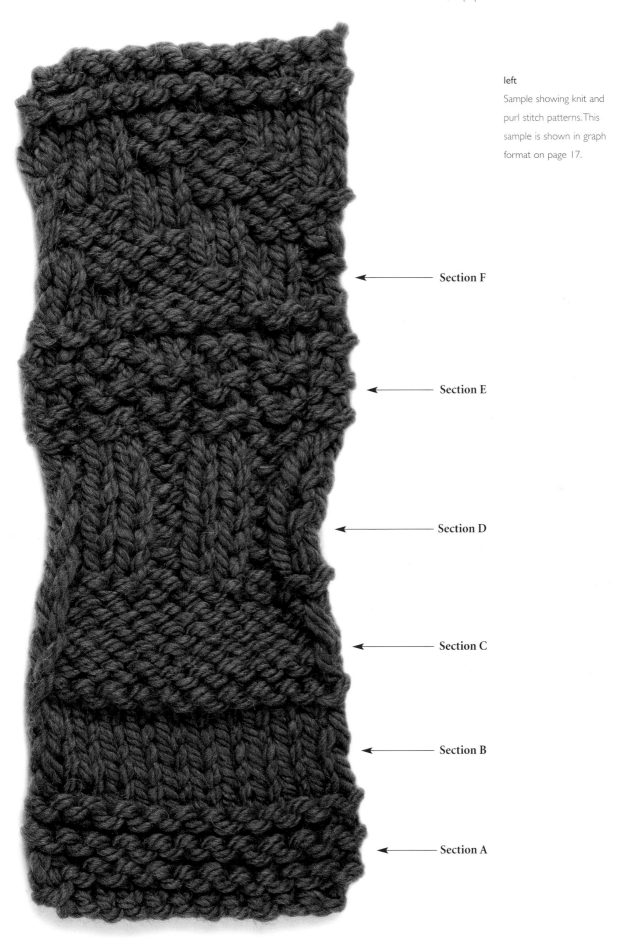

left
Sample showing knit and
purl stitch patterns. This
sample is shown in graph
format on page 17.

Section F

Section E

Section D

Section C

Section B

Section A

remaining stitches are equally divided to the left and the right edges. This pattern, given in knitter's shorthand, is as follows:

Row 1: K4, P4, K4
Row 2: P4, K4, P4
Row 3: P2, K4, P4, K2
Row 4: P2, K4, P4, K2
Row 5: P4, K4, P4
Row 6: K4, P4, K4
Row 7: K2, P4, K4, P2
Row 8: K2, P4, K4, P2

You can repeat these rows as many times as you wish, or knit them once for a border pattern.

Graphs for Knit and Purl Patterns

Instructions in graph form are a universally understood visual language among knitters that eliminates the need for long written patterns. The diagram opposite illustrates the sample on page 15 in graph format.

Odd-numbered rows on the graph are on the right side (facing you) of the work while even-numbered rows are on the wrong side (back) of the work. Read the graph from right to left when working on the right-side rows (odd-numbered), and from left to right for the wrong-side rows (even-numbered). On right-side rows the white squares represent knit stitches, and the black squares are the purl stitches. On wrong-side rows the white squares are purl stitches and the black squares are the knit stitches. Where relevant, the pattern repeat unit is contained within heavy vertical lines.

Abandoning the Written Pattern

Once you have grasped the essential nature of constructing a knitted surface, you will be able to progress to more complex stitch patterns and knitting techniques. As you move on you will find that you can 'draw' with yarn and needles and translate textures and forms in the natural or built world. As the subsequent chapters will show, once you can do this you never need to work from a written pattern again. At the very least you will feel confident in altering a pattern so that it suits your own purposes.

As a precursor to more ambitious knitting, practice knitting various combinations of knit and purl stitches. Move between one and the other but at first keep to the same number of stitches for each row throughout. Experiment with both regular patterns and a more informal approach. Having learned the differences between knit and a purl stitch, you can graph out your designs for future reference.

Practice knitting as if you were sketching on paper, making decisions as to which stitch to work next as you are knitting. Once you feel confident with working with standard-length stitches, move on to elongating stitches and also to introducing spaces into the work. Note down what you do as you knit, using these initial explorations as a jumping-off point for further focused experimentation.

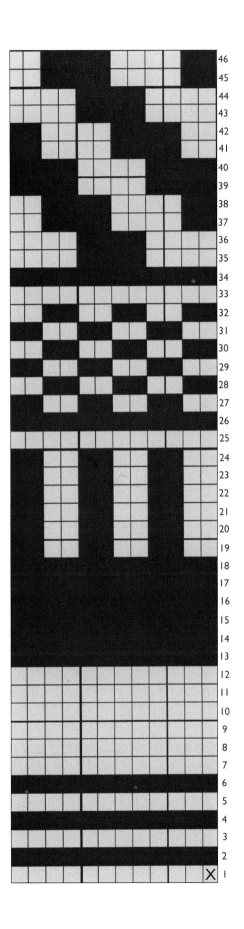

46
45
44
43
42
41
40
39
38
37
36
35
34
33
32
31
30
29
28
27
26
25
24
23
22
21
20
19
18
17
16
15
14
13
12
11
10
9
8
7
6
5
4
3
2
1

left

Knitted sample in graph
format, created using Easy
Knit software (see page
15 for completed sample).

   knit stitch
       purl stitch
X   start knitting here

2 Yarns, Fibres and Other Materials

This chapter introduces a variety of different types of linear materials, and invites you to broaden your awareness by working towards a collection of simply constructed knitted samples. It is a good idea to log your findings systematically during this process, to provide a useful resource for future projects.

Yarns, fibres and other less conventional linear materials appeal to both our visual and tactile senses, and speak to the textile artist, designer-maker and viewer on many different levels – for example, as purely decorative or practical properties or for their ability to provoke a particular metaphor, or even an emotional response. The materials with which we knit can create texture, pattern and structure in both two and three dimensions. The expressive properties of materials are important but so are their physical attributes, such as their relative strength, durability and elasticity, or their ability to retain their shape, to absorb and repel moisture, to felt or take dye. Before you can start expressing yourself with fluency and sensitivity as a textile artist you need to have a practical working knowledge of a wide range of materials.

Balls of yarn give little information as to how they will appear once knitted up, so it is a good idea to make a small knitted sample routinely to add to your resources file for future reference. For example, the following pages show a selection of yarns produced from plant fibres, including recycled and eco-friendly yarns knitted in garter stitch, non-traditional knitting yarns, various textures of hair fibres and dry and rigid materials more normally associated with basketry. Indeed, knitting one of these more unusual materials – basket-makers' centre cane – is used as a case study for investigating material properties (see samples on pages 26–27). This chapter also explains techniques for strengthening short lengths of fragile fibres and materials by twisting them together, using fibres from the day lily plant and rough cut muslin fabric (see sample on page 25). Ways of transforming linear materials, such as stitching, and various surface treatments such as painting, colouring, varnishing, burning, distressing, waxing and stiffening are explored later, in chapters 9 and 10.

All commercially manufactured yarns could be described as man-made, but they differ in whether they are produced from naturally occurring substances, synthesized from chemicals, or from a combination of both. In relation to yarns and textiles, natural materials are those harvested from plant, animal or mineral sources.

right

Circular form knitted in paper string and transparent tape.

Plant-Derived Fibres

Historically, plant-derived materials have been used by indigenous cultures to produce baskets, cordage (ropes, strings and bindings) and textiles. Flax, for example, is thought to have been in cultivation for around 10,000 years, and was used to make the linen fabric that wrapped Egyptian mummies as a symbol of light and purity. Hemp is another of the oldest and most versatile plant fibres, with its use in textiles dating from at least 6,000 years ago, in China, and spreading to Asia and Europe.

The useful fibres in plants are obtained from the leaves, stems and stalks, from the inner bark of tree trunks and the seed heads of plants. Cotton is produced from the fibres that grow inside the cotton boll (seed pod). In particular, yarns and cordage made from bast fibres are strong and durable, and found in the stalk of plants such as hemp (*Cannabis sativa*), flax (*Linum usitatissimum*), nettle (*Urtica cannabina*), kenaf, ramie and jute.

Raffia and banana palms, pineapple plants (bromeliads) and the New Zealand flax (*Phormium tenax*) are all used for their fibrous leaves. The long fibres of the raffia palm leaf are stripped into lengths to make raffia, a strong yet soft material that knits more easily if dampened before use. Currently made in Nepal from materials recycled from weaving mill waste, banana silk yarn is described as 100 per cent rayon (meaning it is made from regenerated cellulose using modern chemical techniques). It is dyed in a range of colours or solid shades (for availability and colour ranges see Suppliers, page 124).

Other plant-based materials include paper yarns, and tapes spun from paper that, in turn, is processed from wood fibres. Japanese paper yarn, for example, is made from Washi paper that is produced from the long inner fibres of the Kozo, Mitsumata and Gampi plants. I suggest the following needle sizes for various types of paper yarns: 25mm (US size 50) and 5.5mm (US size 9) needles for corded paper yarns, 4, 15 and 25mm (US sizes 6, 19 and 50) needles for the various flat-profile tape yarns and 2.75mm (US size 2) needles for fine paper string.

Nearer to home, domestic gardens and local hedgerows can also yield a surprising range of materials that have potential as a knitting medium, including the strong, pliable stems used as weavers in basketry. For example, climbers and trailing plants such as clematis, honeysuckle, hops, ivy and the long, strap-like leaves of the day lily (*Hemerocallis*) can all provide unusual materials for knitting as art. Always seek permission to harvest materials where appropriate.

This sample (right) shows examples of yarns derived from plant fibres including banana silk on 4.5mm (US size 7) needles, recycled sari yarns on 7mm (US size 10¾) needles, Kashmir sari ribbon on 4–5mm (US size 6–8) needles and Tansing tweed on 7.5mm (US 10⅞) needles, which is 60 per cent recycled rayon and 40 per cent New Zealand wool.

below

Samples knitted in commercially produced plant fibre yarn. From top: bamboo, hand-dyed paper yarn, cornstarch, banana silk, recycled sari yarn and Kashmir sari ribbon, Tansing tweed.

This sample (right) shows that plant material more usually associated with basketry has great potential for sculptural knitting. For example, centre cane or reed that is processed from the pithy centre of rattan (*Calmoideae* family), knitted on 4.5mm (US size 7) and 10–12mm (US size 15–17) wooden needles. Also shown here is sisal garden twine knitted on size 6mm (US size 10) wooden needles, raffia on 6mm (US size 10) and 8mm (US size 11) wooden needles, and Nepalese hand-spun nettle yarn on 4mm (US size 6) bamboo needles.

Animal Fibres

Examples of animal-hair fibres include wool from various breeds of sheep – for example Merino, Shetland and Icelandic – and also lambswool, which is the first soft clip from lambs less than six months old. Other fibres in this category include cashmere, llama, alpaca, camel and yak hair, musk ox fibres, the silky lustrous fibres from the Angora goat (mohair) and Angora hair from the rabbits of the same name.

This sample (below) shows examples of undyed hair fibres in a variety of textures and weights. Suggested needle sizes for these fibres: rovings (loose, untwisted fibres) – 25mm (US size 50), Texere bouclé – 5.5mm (US size 9), Rowan Biggy Print – 20mm (US size 35), loop mohair – 9mm (US size 13), Texere slub yarn – 15mm (US size 19), woollen spun – 15mm (US size 19) and Jaeger extra-fine merino – 4mm (US size 6). See page 22 for references to commercially produced and hand-dyed wool and to other natural fibre yarns (also see details at www.colinette.com).

above

Knitted samples worked in (from top) raffia, hand-spun nettle yarn, sisal and centre cane.

below

Various weights and textures of hair fibres.

Luxury Fibres

Silk is a fine, soft fibre, a product of the protein fibre extruded and spun by the silk moth larvae to make its cocoon. The most commonly used moth for producing silk is the *Bombyx mori*, or Chinese silkworm, which feeds off the Mulberry tree. In traditional silk production, or sericulture, the fibre is processed before the moth leaves the cocoon. However, in organic silk production the fibres are not processed until the moth, usually the tussah moth, has vacated, making it more appealing to the ecologically minded. Tussah silk, also known as wild silk, has a rougher texture than the smooth sheen of reeled silk.

Synthetic Materials

Synthetic materials made from chemical substances include viscose rayon, polyester, nylon, polyamides, elastics, acrylics, Lycra, Spandex and Lurex – as well as the new generation of high-tech performance fabrics manufactured from microfibres. Of interest to the fibre artist are specialist fibres, such as UV colour-changing thread, reflective yarns made of thousands of minute glass beads, or similar yarns that incorporate dissolvable fibres for ease of use.

Mineral Sources

Mineral sources for fibres include asbestos, glass fibres, metal and oil. Stainless steel and copper are used in modern yarn design, the latter sometimes wrapped with merino wool – the stainless steel gives the yarn a 'memory' effect, so that the textile retains its shape until straightened out.

Ethical Considerations

Ethical considerations may affect your choice of material. For example, you may prefer to use organically grown eco-friendly cotton, silk and hemp fibres that use chemical-free production processes and exploit naturally occurring vegetable or mineral dyes or low-impact dyeing methods and sun bleaching.

If you use Fair Trade yarn you can be confident that the workers involved in the yarn's production have received a fair price for their efforts (for example, see the yarns available from www.frabjousfibers.com). By using their traditional skills people in places like Nepal are able to support themselves and their families. You could also consider knitting with biodegradable materials, such as the GM-free cornstarch used in the manufacture of carrier bags. If you use these in temporary environmentally friendly outdoor art works they will eventually compost down over a period of time.

Examples of some of the new generation, eco-friendly natural yarns currently on the market include Pure, which is 100 per cent Soysilk, bamboo yarn and 100 per cent corn-fibre yarns, such as Amaizing or Cornucopia, all of which are available from the South West Trading

Company (SWTC) and other outlets. Bamboo and Soysilk yarns are silky to the touch, whereas the corn-fibre tape yarns feel similar to soft cotton with a matt appearance. Suggested needle size for these types of yarn: bamboo – 4mm (US size 6), 2 strands 100 per cent Soysilk – 4–6mm (US size 6–10), Cornucopia – 4.5mm (US size 7), Gianna (50 per cent Soysilk and 50 per cent wool) – 6.5mm (US size 10½).

Unconventional Knitting Mediums

The samples in this book use many unconventional linear knitting mediums. This sample (right) shows a small selection of potential materials, with an indication of suitable needle sizes and types. All examples are knitted in garter stitch.

Black marine rope knitted on 15mm (US size 19) needles; dress/tutu net on 7mm (US size 10¾) wooden needles; single-core bell wire on 15mm (US size 19) strong plastic needles. Also included is 6.5mm (¼in) flat-profile, black lingerie elastic knitted on size 7mm (US size 10¾) wooden needles. Note that a 4.5m (14.8ft) length of this type of elastic knitted a very small sample of only 10 rows and 8 stitches but does combine very well with black marine rope to produce a really solid fabric, suited to bag making. This group of samples is completed by examples of recycled plastics made from GM-free cornstarch biodegradable bags on size 6mm (US size 10) wooden needles and, finally, handmade cordage knitted on large wooden needles, also produced from carrier bags.

right

Examples of non-traditional knitting media. From top: lingerie elastic, tutu net, carrier bags, single-core bell wire, GM-free plastic and marine rope.

Consider experimenting with some of the hard-to-knit transparent media and plastics, for example 2mm (1⁄16in) monofilament, deep-sea fishing line on 20mm (US size 35) needles, polypropylene tape on 3.75mm (US size 5) bamboo needles, fishing line on 4mm (US size 6) needles and strimmer cord on 6.5mm (US size 10½) needles. Note that some of these materials knit up with a bias or have a tendency to curl at the edges, even in garter stitch. Bubble wrap and cling film (Saran wrap) also have the potential for softer more pliable surfaces and are easily knitted on large wooden needles.

Other alternative knitting materials include video and audio tape, horticultural fleece cut in strips, strips of fabric, ribbons, tapes, shirring elastic, rubber bands, ribbons, threads and yarns, and Tyvek. Recycled telephone cable and Day-Glo synthetic garden string are also worth exploring (try size 6mm (US size 10) wooden needles), as is plastic-coated 1mm (1⁄32in) tying wire on 12mm (US size 17) plastic needles and enamelled copper wire – 0.315mm available from The Scientific Wire Company – knitted on 4mm (US size 6) metal needles.

Commercially Produced Yarns

Throughout the book, yarns from the smaller specialist companies have been chosen for sampling purposes, in particular those from Colinette Yarns. This company carries a wide range of top-quality yarns that are also hand dyed in the same colour ranges. For example, various textures and wools available include pure new wool Point 5, merino four-ply and DK, mohair and wool mix, cotton and wool mix, kid mohair, rayon and cotton mixes, pure cotton and 100 per cent luxury silk.

Texere Yarns (www.texere.co.uk) also carries a wide range of fibres, textures and colours in dyed and undyed yarns: for example alpaca, cotton, cashmere, linen, metallic yarns, mohair, silk, viscose and wool. New Zealand-based Yarn Traders (www.yarntraders.co.nz) have a good range of exotic, natural yarns including banana silk, Kashmiri silk ribbon and Tansing tweed. In the United States, banana silk (100 per cent rayon), recycled silk, recycled cotton, rayon and blends, natural fibres such as nettle, hemp and Charka cotton are available in a stunning range of colours from Frabjous Fibers (www.frabjousfibers.com). Also of interest for felting is Rowan Scottish Tweed pure wool, produced using traditional spinning and dyeing techniques. More information on suppliers is included at the end of the book.

Making and Preparing Materials

Some fibres and materials are robust enough to knit without further processing but you can also turn more fragile materials into surprisingly strong handmade yarns and cordage.

Making Two-Ply Cordage

Using a simple tried-and-trusted method you can create strong string and cordage by twisting together a bundle of more fragile fibres. First select a bundle of fibres, leaves or rags and tie a knot in one end. Attach one end of a piece of string to the knot and the other end to a doorknob, keeping the bundled fibres under tension. (Once the rope you are creating is long enough you could sit on the floor with your legs outstretched, and use your feet to hold the fibres under tension, or you could sit on the end of the newly twisted rope.)

Keep a bowl of water nearby to moisten your hands and/or the fibres. Divide the bundle in half, and take one half of the bundle in your right hand and the other in your left. Keeping the bundles under tension, roll the fibres in your right hand away from the body between the thumb and the forefinger for three twists (for example). Bring the twisted fibres in the right hand over the bundle of fibres in the left hand, locking the newly formed twist in place.

Next, swap the bundles over so that you are now holding the bundle you have just twisted in your left hand, keeping the bundles under tension all the time. Continue this rolling, locking and swapping process, adding in new lengths of plant (or other) material as the old ones run out. Try to stagger the joins, tapering the ends of the new additions.

Other methods of making cordage include rolling the fibres between the thighs and the palms of the hands. Basketry manuals are a good source for techniques.

This sample (below) shows hand-made yarns and knitted samples made from the long, strap-like leaves of the day lily plant on 3.75mm (US size 5) needles, and rough-cut strips of white muslin on 5–7mm (US size 8–10¾) needles. You can do the same with strips of recycled fabrics and strips of plastic carrier bags.

below

Making your own cordage takes you back to basics and, once knitted up, your cordage produces unique results.

Twisting Yarns

Custom-made yarn twisters are available, while a less sophisticated method involves using a door handle or hand drill. Other options for handmade yarns include plying yarns together on the spinning wheel and using the braiding foot on the domestic sewing machine to make textured yarns.

Knitting Unfamiliar Materials

Before embarking on a major piece of work in unfamiliar materials, test out their behaviour and properties in some depth, and record your findings carefully in a notebook. Basket-making rattan is used as an example here.

Working with short lengths of fibres or inflexible materials such as rattan, the first hurdles to overcome are finding a way of turning it into a continuous length of yarn, or cordage, and making it flexible enough to knit with. Hard, inflexible or brittle natural materials such as this need to be prepared for knitting as you would for making a basket. A few rules of thumb for working with cane follow, but you should refer to basketry books for information on specific plant materials.

Commercially available material, such as processed cane, requires very little preparation other than soaking and mellowing (see below), and should be flexible and not crack or break when in use. Manufactured from the pithy centre of rattan, centre cane is very porous, and easily soaked to make it pliable, and also receptive to dyeing if required.

below
Dyed and varnished
knitted basketry cane.

First soak the cane for up to ten minutes (depending upon size), coiled loosely in a bowl. *Do not over soak the cane* as it will discolour and the grain will raise. Remove the cane from the bowl and shake off any excess of wetness, then wrap it in a damp towel to mellow it. This simply means allowing the remaining moisture to penetrate right through to the centre of the material, making it less likely to snap when woven or knitted. Try not to prepare more cane than you need at any one time. If you do have leftover materials store them so that air can get to them: if you wrap cane in a plastic bag it will eventually go mouldy.

To test if the cane is flexible enough to knit, try to make crochet chains. Due to the hard nature of the material you will probably need to use a much larger hook than you expect. But experiment with a range of hook and needle sizes – from the smallest you can knit with to a really large size – in order to establish a range of useful tensions suitable to the material, its intended end use, and the look of the knitting. No one tension works for all types of stitch structure, even when using the same material, so test different types of needles and methods of holding the needles with your chosen knitting medium.

These samples (above and opposite) show a selection of experiments knitted in dyed, stained and varnished centre cane. The latter is worked in the same manner as the wire edgings shown in chapter 4 while the sample on the following page illustrates installation work for outdoor settings, created by the author and knitted in the same material.

above

Experimental samples in basketry cane. Try using various thicknesses of cane and explore dyeing and varnishing techniques.

above

Hand knitted installation in
undyed basketry cane.

Tension Swatches

Conventional balls of yarn indicate the number of rows and stitches required to knit a 10cm
(4in) square on a given needle size. But at some point you are bound to need to know how to
calculate the number of rows and stitches required for a particular shape in a non-standard
material. The information below describes how to calculate this from a tension swatch that you
have made – and there is really no substitute for this if you want to knit materials to a particular,
predictable size.

Tension (or gauge) refers to the number of rows and stitches for a given measurement.
Different needle sizes, thickness of material and type of stitch patterns all knit up to very
different tensions (see the wool samples from two-ply through to unspun fleece shown on page
21). A 10cm (4in) square knitted in rope will require a different number of rows and stitches to
the same size knitted in fine linen thread. Basically, the thicker the knitting medium the fewer
the rows and stitches needed, assuming the same stitch pattern.

Whatever knitting medium you are using, you will need to knit a tension swatch (or similar)
in the yarn, needle size and stitch pattern that you intend to use for the finished piece. This will
give you a clear indication of how many rows and stitches the complete piece will require. The
method of calculating rows and stitches for any given measurement is given below. It can be
used or tweaked when working with non-traditional materials, or with patterns that do not
repeat at regular intervals across the knitting. And the same principle applies whether you are
knitting a massive piece for a gallery installation or small-scale body adornment.

Method:

1. Cast on 20 stitches in the main knitting medium (A), knit for 4 rows, knit 2 rows in a
   contrasting colour or fibre (B), and 10 rows in A.
2. Insert a tie marker on the 6th and 15th stitch as you knit the next row. Knit a further 10
   rows in A, 2 rows in B, and 4 rows in A. Cast off.

For standard knitting yarns:

3. Using a squared blocking board, pin the swatch out so that the edges are parallel to each other. Cover with a cotton cloth and steam press (unless the ball band of the yarn states that you must not do this, in which case simply measure, as described below). Obviously you will not be able to block the square in this way for many of the more unconventional knitting materials discussed in this book.

Remember, the aim is to work out how many stitches and rows you will need to knit a 10cm (4in) square.

*   First, measure the swatch flat between the tie markers. This will give you a measurement for 10 stitches – for example 15cm (6in).
*   To find the number of stitches per cm (⅜in), divide 10 (the number of stitches) by this measurement. The result will be the tension for 1cm (⅜in). This example will give you a tension of 0.61 stitches to 1cm (⅜in) or – by multiplying 0.61 by 10 – around **6 whole stitches per 10cm** (4in).

*   Now measure the distance between the top and bottom rows of contrast colours. For example 20 rows may measure 20cm (8in).
*   To find out what 1cm equals in terms of rows, divide the number of rows by the number of cm – in this case 20 rows divided by 20cm (8in). In this example the result will give you a tension of 1 row per 1cm (0.4in). From this you can see that **10 rows takes 10cm** (4in) – 1 (cm) multiplied by 10.

You can conclude that, in this example, a 10cm (4in) square is therefore 6 stitches by 10 rows. With this information you can calculate the number of rows and stitches needed to knit any given shape. If you are working this out for complex shapes, break them down into their individual primitive shapes first (squares, triangles and rectangles for example) before making these calculations.

To calculate the approximate number of stitches and rows needed to knit a non-repeating pattern in unusual materials, try knitting a small vertical slice, say ten stitches wide or a similar number that is suited to the pattern and knitting medium. Knit as many rows as needed for the complete length of the piece and estimate from this sample.

3 Big Knitting

Inspired by patterns and colour in the landscape, this chapter exploits the differences in appearance between knit- and purl-facing stitches to create textured and dimensional surfaces from scratch. These simple-to-work patterns associated with garment knitting take on a new dimension when removed from their normal context and knitted on a grand scale on large needles. Big knitting of this kind has much potential for floor and wall coverings, non-functional art textiles and, of course, sumptuous outwear and detachable accessories, such as cuffs, collars and head wear.

I will explain techniques for creating ridges and furrows in low and high relief and methods for creating double-faced surfaces on two needles.

Materials suitable for 'big knitting' include traditional yarns, ribbon, recycled fabrics and over-dyed off-the-shelf cottons and viscose, the latter bulked up into chain loops and tubes using crochet, spool and machine knitting techniques.

below

Sample knitted in strips of torn fabric and Colinette Enigma.

Knit- and Purl-Facing Stitch Patterns

The first group of samples in this chapter develop further the basic knit- and purl-facing patterns outlined in chapter 1 (see page 15), now worked in a combination of commercially manufactured yarns (Colinette) and recycled rough-cut fabrics.

The samples on the following pages explore ways of combining recycled fabrics with various textured yarns in knit and purl stitch patterns. A limited colour palette was chosen in order to harmonize these strongly contrasting elements, in the same way that painted textures and marks can be made to work together within an artwork.

The sample opposite is knitted on 10mm (US size 15) plastic needles in a three-row, four-stitch pattern repeat. Torn strips of silky and metallic fabrics in solid colours complement the space-dyed hues of Colinette Enigma. To work a similar swatch, knit one row using fabric plus three ends of yarn, followed by two rows in a knit 2 purl 2 rib without the fabric. Leave the latter attached to the knitting, reintroducing it on every third row, as described above.

The sample below is tightly knitted on 10mm (US size 15) needles to produce a fabric suitable for interior applications. It is constructed from strips of georgette and silk fabric (A), one strand of Colinette Isis (B) and a pre-crocheted and over-dyed chain (C). The latter is made up of several strands of machine-knit-weight viscose and cotton yarn. To knit a similar swatch, cast on in multiples of 6 stitches. Knit 1 row in A, B and C. Knit 3 rows in a knit 3, purl 3 rib in B and C only. Repeat these four rows throughout.

right

Sample knitted in roughly cut strips of fabric and Colinette Isis.

left

Big-scale knitting in
Colinette Isis and Point 5,
combined with fabric strips.

The sample above shows large-scale knitting worked
on 20mm (US size 35) plastic needles from torn strips of
georgette fabric plied with two strands of Colinette Point
5 wool (A) and a four-prong spool-knitted tube (B) in
Colinette Point 5 and Isis. A is knitted for three rows as
a knit 3 purl 3 rib. To compensate for the differences in
weights between A and B, the latter is knitted or purled
on every other stitch only, for one row.

The sample shown right is a knitted in a variety of
large-scale handmade cordage made from
wonderfully textured crochet chains, spool-knitted,
machine-knitted and felted tubes.

right

Sample knitted in
handmade cordage.

above

Knit and purl stitch pattern
knitted in pre-made tubes.

These samples (above and right) are robustly constructed in knit and purl
stitch patterns that were designed to lie flat, and have great potential for floor
coverings. Knitted on 15 and 20mm (US size 19 and 35) needles using
pre-made tubes constructed from multiple ends of fine yarn in
graduating colours (see chapter 2 for information on creating cordage),
the samples are over-dyed to harmonize with the off-the-shelf colours.
The sample opposite shows alternative large-scale handmade cordage.

Note the long, narrow strip knitted on the bias, a technique that offers
much potential for knitting diagonal strips that can be joined together to make large-scale
works. The principle of bias knitting is to increase a stitch at the beginning of the row, followed
by a decrease at the end of the same row. Alternatively, increase a stitch at the beginning of the
row, followed by a decrease at the beginning of the next row.

above

Bias knitted strip made
from pre-made tube.

Ridges and Furrows

The two samples shown right demonstrate different methods of achieving ridges and furrows.

The sample at the top shows horizontal ridges and furrows in alternating bands of knit and purl stocking stitch.

Knit an odd number of rows in stocking stitch (alternating knit and purl rows), starting with a knit row. Repeat this group of rows as many times as required, always beginning and ending with a knit row. Note that every other section is knit-facing stocking stitch, and alternating with purl-facing stocking stitch, sampled here using three strands of Colinette Tagliatelli.

The juxtaposition of two knit rows, following each other and in effect turning the work from front-facing to back-facing stocking stitch, creates the undulating profile of this stitch pattern. This textural finish is more effective over short numbers of rows than with widely spaced bands of knitting.

In the sample at the bottom, you can see pin-tuck ridges, knitted in two strands of Colinette Pont 5 and three ends of Colinette Tagliatelli. This method uses a third needle to link sections of the knitting to form pin tucks.

To make a pin tuck, knit the amount of rows required for the pin tucks in a contrasting colour or texture yarn. Using a third needle, pick up the loops from the first row of the pin tucks, with the point of the needle facing in the same direction as the main working needle – you should have the same number of stitch loops on both needles. Hold both needles parallel to each other. With the remaining needle, knit a stitch from the front needle together with a stitch from the back needle, working all the way along the row.

right

Two samples
showing knitted-in
ridges and furrows.

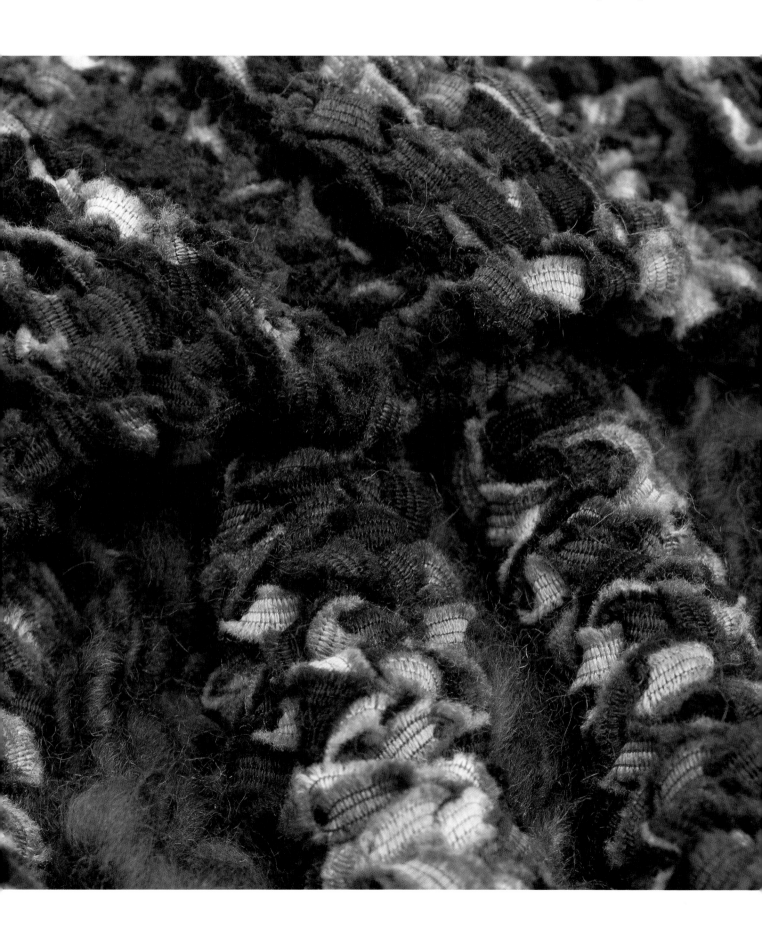

These samples (left and opposite) show slip-stitch patterns, which are a good choice for interior applications, such as floor coverings. Firm to handle, they have limited elasticity and also lie flat. The double-sided knitting shown below right is a sophisticated interpretation of the standard slip-stitch technique.

These samples demonstrate the basic principles of slip-stitch knitting before moving on to the more complex stitch structures of doubled-sided fabrics. The sample on the left is knitted on 10mm (US size 15) needles over 15 stitches in a single end of Colinette Point 5 yarn (B) and two ends of Skye pure wool (A). The swatch could be used on either side.

1. Knit 2 rows A. Leave yarn attached.
2. Change to B. * Knit 1, slip 1 purl-wise with the yarn at the *back* of the knitting *. Repeat from * to * until 1 stitch remains. Knit 1.
3. Knit the stitches you knitted in B on the previous row and slip purl-wise all the other stitches, bringing the yarn forward *between the needles* as you do so. You will need to take the yarn to the back each time to make the knit stitch.
4. Repeat these 4 rows, three times in all, changing colours every 2 rows.
5. Knit 2 rows A.
6. Change to B. * Knit 1, slip 1 purl-wise with the yarn at the *front* of the knitting, take the yarn to the back of the knitting *. Repeat from * to * until 1 stitch remains. Knit 1.
7. Knit the stitches you knitted in B on the previous row and slip purl-wise all the other stitches with the yarn *at the back of the knitting.*

left

Multicoloured slip-stitch knitting.

8. Variations include repeating steps 2 and 3 twice, three or four times, before knitting two rows on all stitches. Notice how the long vertical floats in A become a separate layer until they are finally knitted-in at the completion of the slip-stitch section. Notice also that if you repeat steps 6 and 7 in the same manner as just described then the knitting is reversed so that the long stitches are on the opposite side of the work.

9. The ridges form on the side where the extra rows have been knitted. Ridges can be knitted in stocking stitch by purling the stitches in steps 3 or 7 thus: *purl* the stitches you knitted in B on the previous row, and slip purl-wise all the other stitches with the yarn *at the back of the knitting for the slip-stitch and brought forward between the needles to work the purl stitch*.

below

This piece was developed from the sample shown opposite.

Double-Sided Knitting

above

Tubular-knitted, double-
faced surface in Colinette
Point 5, stuffed with
coloured rovings.

By using various combinations of knit, purl and slipped stitches, it is possible to knit two
independent layers of fabric at the same time on a single pair of straight or double-pointed
needles. The two layers can be connected at any point, then opened out again into two separate
layers. Ridges and short tunnels can be incorporated into the work on either side of the fabric.

Knitting Two Unconnected Layers

Cast on 15 stitches in colour A plus colour B – that is, each stitch loop comprises two strands of
yarn. Leave both colours attached to the knitting.

> **Row 1:** change to colour A and knit only the loops in colour A, slipping the loops in colour
> B thus: * Knit 1, bring the yarn to the front of the knitting in between the needles and slip
> 1 purl-wise. Take the yarn to the back of the knitting *. Repeat from * to * until all stitches
> have been knitted in this manner. 15 stitches in A and 15 stitches in B remain.
>
> **Row 2:** continue to knit in colour A. Purl the 15 stitches in A that you have just knitted and
> slip the 15 slipped stitches in B from the previous row thus: * Take the yarn to the back of
> the knitting, slip 1 purl-wise, return the yarn to the front of the knitting between the
> needles, purl 1, *. Repeat from * to * until all stitches have been knitted in this manner.
> 15 stitches in A and 15 stitches in B remain.
>
> **Row 3:** change to colour B and knit only the loops in B thus: knit the stitches that you
> slipped on rows 1 and 2 and slip all the other stitches (in A) purl-wise, with the yarn at the
> back of the knitting.
>
> **Row 4:** continue to knit in colour B. Purl the stitches you have just knitted in row 3, and slip
> all the other stitches (in A) purl-wise, with the yarn to the front of the knitting.

These four rows form the pattern repeat. One side of the work is knit-facing and the other
purl-facing. To knit a similar fabric, but with the outer sides of both layers knit-facing, work
as follows:

Rows 1 and 2: as above.

Row 3: change to colour B and purl only the loops in B thus: purl the stitches that you slipped on rows 1 and 2 and slip all the other stitches (A), with the yarn placed at the back of the knitting.

Row 4: continue to knit in colour B. Knit all the stitches you have just knitted in row 3 and slip all the other stitches (A) purl-wise with the yarn to the front of the knitting.

Joining the layers: * Slip 1 purl-wise with the yarn at the front. Purl 1 *. Repeat from * to * until all stitches have been knitted in this manner. Repeat this row twice in A. Work another section of tubular knitting as described above, but this time commencing with colour B.

The sample opposite is knitted in Colinette Pont 5 and shows tubular knitted layers connected and separated, the latter being stuffed with coloured rovings.

The sample below shows slip-stitch ridges. To make these pronounced ridges knit extra rows on one half of the stitches to produce a longer length of knitting than on the under layer. Connect both layers with joining rows, as described above, and alternate ridges with flat double-sided tubular knitting. In this example the latter was felted after the knitting had been completed and stuffed with coloured rovings. When working, insert bubble wrap or similar between the open layers so that they don't felt together.

below

Felted, double-faced tubular knitting.

Ridge Pattern

Row 1: * knit 1, bring the yarn forward between the needles, slip
1 stitch purl-wise, return the yarn to the back of the knitting *.
Repeat from * to * until all stitches have been knitted in
this way.

Row 2: * with the yarn at the back of the work, slip 1
stitch purl-wise, bring the yarn forward between the
needles. Purl 1 stitch *. Repeat from * to * until all
stitches have been worked in this way.

Repeat rows 1 and 2 until the depth of the ridge is
knitted. Knit 2 linking rows followed by a section of
tubular knitting.

Further experiments with double-sided knitting
might include layers of different types of stitch patterns,
for example rib and stocking stitch or thin yarns over
thick yarns. Extreme variations of tension and/or yarn
thickness between the two layers will inevitably distort the outer
edges of the fabric.

Complex Structures in Slip-Stitch Patterns

Knitted in Colinette Pont 5, this example is constructed using a combination of knit- and
purl-facing tubular knitting, with a central strip of two stitches worked in all rows as knit.
Challenging to knit, the structures are a patchwork of interconnected blocks of knit- and
purl-facing double-layered stitch patterns.

Cast on 16 stitches in two colours, as described above, so that you have 16 stitches in colours
A and 16 in colour B. The first section of the swatch is knitted thus:

Row 1: work in colour A. * Knit 1, slip 1 stitch with yarn forward *. Repeat from * to * 7
times in total. Knit 2 stitches. ** Purl 1, slip 1 with the yarn at the back **. Repeat from ** to
** 7 times in total.

Row 2: continue in colour A. * With the yarn at the back of the knitting, slip 1 stitch, knit
1 *. Repeat from * to * 7 times in total. Knit 2 stitches. ** With the yarn at the back of the
knitting, slip 1 stitch, purl 1 **. Repeat from ** to ** 7 times in total.

Row 3: change to colour B. * With the yarn at the back of the knitting, slip 1 stitch, purl 1 *.
Repeat from * to * 7 times in total. Knit 2 stitches. ** With the yarn at the front of the
knitting, slip 1 stitch, purl 1 **. Repeat from ** to **7 times in total.

Row 4: continue in colour B. * Knit 1, slip 1 stitch with the yarn at the back of the knitting *.
Repeat from * to * 7 times in total. Knit 2 stitches. ** Knit 1, slip 1 stitch with the yarn at the
front of the knitting **. Repeat from ** to ** 7 times in total.

The swatch continues in this fashion, alternating closed sections with tubular knitting and
making changes to the locations of knit- and purl-facing sections.

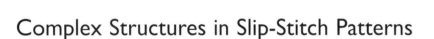

above

Double-faced tubular
knitting in Colinette
Point 5 yarn creates a
complex structure.

Practical Considerations

Consider how best to handle knitting large-scale heavy items. In practical terms try to develop
designs that can be knitted in modules and then connected together on completion of the
knitting. If this is not possible, stand up to knit, using a table to take the weight of the work
as it progresses. In extreme cases devise a way of suspending the work as you work. It is most
important not to do permanent damage to hands and shoulders (for more on health and safety
issues, see chapter 1).

4 Borderlines

This chapter explores methods for creating shaped edgings, boundaries and borders in two dimensions. These borders can be applied to existing surfaces and forms or made into free-standing objects. Inspired by microscopic sea creatures such as corals, or the cellular structures of sea sponges, octopus and sea anemone, the edges and borders described below are created from single pattern units that are repeated many times over to build quite intricate structures. Potential applications range from jewellery to window dressing and outdoor screening.

I shall introduce techniques for creating shape and form as an integral part of the knitting process and include short-row knitting techniques, inventive uses of casting on and off, working with multiple increases and decreases and knitted in extensions and add-ons. The techniques are sampled here on different scales, from fine enamelled copper wire mixed with metallic threads through to basket-makers' rattan and paper tape, alongside more traditional yarns. The sideways-knitted borders described here exploit casting on and off techniques, combined with openwork and textured stitch patterns.

below

'Whirpool' knitted in white paper yarn and stiffened with PVA.

left
Large-scale fronds knitted in paper tape.

below
Fronds knitted in white paper string.

Openwork Stitch Patterns

Openwork stitch patterns can be used for knitting frond-like extensions, and often feature single or double eyelets. To form an eyelet, knit to the point where you want the eyelet, bring the yarn from the back, round the needle to the front (as if about to make a purl stitch). Insert the right-hand needle into the loop on the left hand, then take the yarn to the back, ready to knit the next stitch. To compensate for the extra loop created you will need to decrease one stitch, either before or after the made stitch.

A simple eyelet pattern of two stitches would read as follows: * Knit two together, make 1 *. To knit a row of eyelets in this manner cast on any number of stitches divisible by two, for example 24 plus 4 edge stitches so that the row doesn't end on a made stitch. The pattern would read: Knit 2, * knit 2 together, make 1 * repeat from * to * until 2 stitches remain. Knit 2.

Knitting larger enclosed eyelets involves one made stitch and two decreases, made either side of the made stitch: * Knit 2 together, make 1, slip 1, knit 1, pass the slip-stitch over *. On the next row, to compensate for the two decreases in this pattern, you should first purl into the front of the made stitch and then knit into the back of the made stitch, turning the latter into two stitches, so forming the eyelet.

If you are knitting stitch patterns such as these with wire you might find that a slightly larger needle size than normal is necessary in order to be able to knit two stitches together with ease, for example 3mm (US size 2½) instead of 2mm (US size 0) (see sample, right).

Casting On and Off and Elongated Stitches

Your method of casting on and off will depend on the materials you are using. Always test each new knitting medium to discover the most appropriate method. For example, when knitting with wire, casting back on to begin a new frond is best worked with two needles. The samples described below use casting on and off to form border patterns.

To form a twisted elongated stitch, insert your needle into each stitch across a row, wrap yarn around both needles, then wrap yarn around right needle, knit or purl last wrap through the stitch and extra wrap.

This sample (right) is branching fronds knitted in twisted elongated stitch in 0.315mm wire on 2.75–3mm (US size 2–2½) steel needles with a straight edge at top of border.

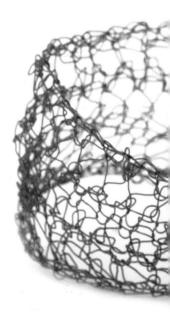

Cast on 34 stitches and knit 1 row.

1. * Knit one row of twisted elongated stitch where the first stitch of the row is a
    standard-length knit stitch.

2. Knit one row normal length *.

3. Repeat from * to * once more.

4. Repeat step 1.

5. Cast off 8 stitches and knit to the end of the row. 26 stitches remain.

6. Repeat step 1 to end of row, casting back on 8 stitches using the two-needle method. You now have 34 stitches.

7. Knit 1 row.

8. Repeat steps 1 to 4 inclusive.

9. Repeat step 1.

10. Cast off 24 stitches and knit to the end of the row. 10 stitches remain.

11. Repeat steps 1 to 3 inclusive on these 10 stitches.

12. Repeat step 1 to end of row, casting back on 24 stitches using the two-needle method. You now have 34 stitches. Knit 1 row.

13. Repeat the first 12 steps as many times as required.

below

Openwork stitch pattern

knitted in wire.

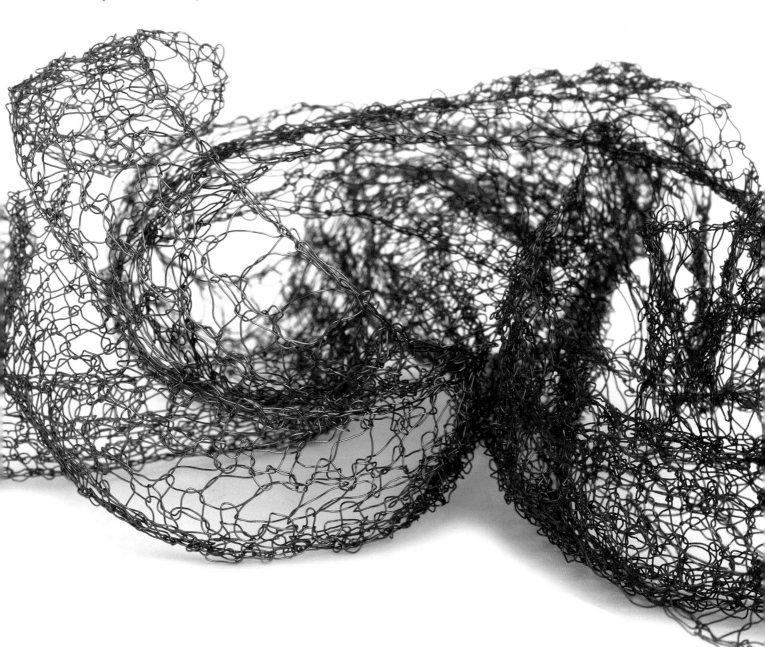

This sample (below) is knitted in 0.315cm enamelled copper wire on 2.75–3mm (US size 2–2½) steel knitting needles, and the pattern is based on a combination of elongated and normal length stitches.

1. Using 2.75–3mm (US size 2–2½) needles cast on 43 stitches and knit 1 row.
2. Knit 2 rows.
3. Knit 1 row of elongated stitches.
4. Knit 3 rows.
5. Knit 1 row of elongated stitches.
6. Repeat steps 4 to 5 once more.
7. Repeat step 2.
8. Cast off 33 stitches and knit the remaining 10 stitches.
9. Knit 10 stitches and cast back on 31 stitches.
10. Repeat steps 2 to 8 as many times as required.
11. Repeat steps 2 to 7 once more.
12. Cast off all 43 stitches.

left

Fronds knitted in copper wire using the technique described above.

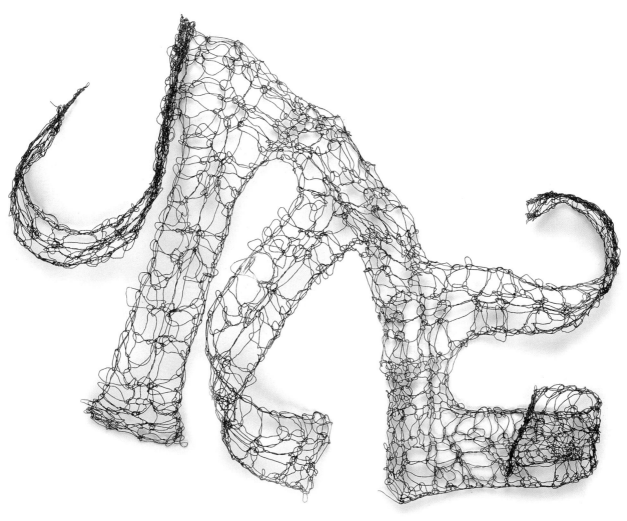

above

Left- and right-facing
fronds.

Many variations on this pattern are possible; for example, on the second repeat of the pattern you can cast off and on 16 stitches at steps 5 and 6. Knitting more, or fewer, rows will alter the width of the frond and more, or fewer, stitches will change the length. Using standard stitches on the border, and elongated stitches on the fronds, would be another variation. Incorporate sections of short-row knitting to curve the straight edge (see page 48). Alternatively, knit the fronds so that some point to the left and the others to the right.

The sample above shows fronds to the left and the right knitted in a combination of twisted elongated stitch and large eyelets. To make a similar swatch, add in an extra row at the end of the pattern sequence so that the new casting-on points in the opposite direction to the previous frond.

Short-Row Knitting

Short-row knitting simply means that you knit only part of the way across a row and turn, before knitting back across some or all of the stitches you have just knitted. The stitches that are not being knitted are held in waiting on the needles, ready to be incorporated back into the knitting in future rows.

Traditionally used to knit darts and heel turnings, this is a really useful technique for creating sculptural effects, or to introduce wedge shapes in contrasting patterns and colours into the knitting. It is also effective for making curves and frilled edges. My examples are inspired by the shapes of coral and sea sponges. (See also chapter 8 for more pattern-knitting techniques.)

The sample below is knitted in two strands of Colinette Fandango on 10mm (US size 15) needles. To create maximum sculptural effects choose a knitting medium with plenty of body, and knit on a fairly tight tension.

Wavy Edges

To form this kind of edge cast on 8 stitches (for example) and knit 2 rows.

1. On the next row knit 5 stitches, leaving 3 stitches that have not been knitted on the left-hand needle.
2. Turn the work and purl back 5 stitches.
3. Knit back and forth on these 5 stitches in stocking stitch for 6 rows, ending on a purl row – so that all of the stitches are on one needle and you have reached the side where you commenced knitting.
4. Now knit on all 8 stitches for 4 rows before making another frilled section on the same edge of the knitting, as before. Alternatively, knit an extra row to take you to the opposite edge of the work for the next frilled section.

Further experiments in knitting wavy edges might involve altering the number of rows and/or stitches for the short-row section, or knitting this section in all knit (garter stitch) or in a broken rib pattern, for example. The straight section could be made longer and knitted in a textured stitch pattern, and the pattern could, of course, be knitted over a greater number of stitches than suggested here.

Ripples

To create a rippled edge, cast on 8 stitches as before and knit 2 rows.

1. Knit 6 stitches, leaving 2 stitches that have not been knitted on the left-hand needle.
2. Turn the work and purl back 4 stitches again, leaving 2 stitches that have not been knitted at the end of this row.
3. Now knit back and forth in stocking stitch on the middle 4 stitches for a further 6 rows, ending on a purl row.
4. On the next row knit the 4 stitches you have just been knitting, followed by the remaining 2 stitches on the left-hand needle.
5. On the next row knit all 8 stitches.
6. Knit a further two rows on all 8 stitches.
7. Repeat steps 1–6 as many times as required.

For further experiments, you might try varying the height, width and placement of the raised area, which in practice means making alterations to the number of stitches cast on, the number of rows between each raised area and the number of rows worked for the latter.

Wedge Shapes

Knitted in the same manner as a dart, these triangular wedge-shaped insertions are repeated one after the other to create a curved edge. You can combine wedge shapes with ripples and ridges.

left

Short-row knitting sample, knitted in wavy edges (left), ripples (centre) and wedge shapes (right).

To make a flat wedge, you need gradually to increase or decrease the number of stitches knitted on every alternate row on the short-row sections. In the example given below, the wedge is knitted on progressively fewer stitches.

1. Cast on 8 stitches as before.
2. Knit all 8 stitches and purl back 8 stitches.
3. Knit 6 stitches, turn and purl back these 6 stitches.
4. Knit 4 stitches, turn and purl back these 4 stitches.
5. Knit 2 stitches, turn and purl back these 2 stitches.
6. Now knit all 8 stitches for 4 rows (for example) before making the next wedge shape.

Note that there is a row of eyelets created at the points where you have knitted and turned. See the information on pattern knitting in chapter 8 for further information on this technique, and in particular for methods of disguising the holes (see page 99).

below

Detail of short row knitting sample (see page 48). Knitted in Colinette Fandango, cotton chenille yarn.

The sample above is hand-painted paper braid in short-row knitting techniques. This piece was knitted in white paper tape and then painted with acrylic inks.

The sample below is machine-knitted in fine wire and Madeira embroidery thread, using knit and turn short-row techniques. It was inspired by cellular structures, with a delicate sculptural effect where the centre raised sections stand proud of the outside edges. The sample on page 45 shows a hand-knit version of this technique. You could wear this kind of sample around the neck, or use it as an edging.

above

Hand-painted paper braid.

below

Machine-knitted ripples.

Add-Ons

Add-ons are knitted either as separate sections, or units,
and placed on a stitch holder until required or as
continuous lengths of edgings. They are subsequently
incorporated into the main body of the work as the
knitting progresses.

Here, five frilled sections were knitted separately and
stored on a stitch holder or circular needle until needed.
Knitted in the same colour-way in contrasting textures of
two strands of Colinette Enigma (colour A), one strand of
Fandango (colour B) and two strands of Isis (colour C), on
7.5mm (US size 10⅞) needles.

To make this frilled edging, proceed as follows:

1. Cast on 24 stitches in B and knit 2 rows each of B, A
    and B (6 rows in total).
2. Knit 1 row in A.
3. On the next row knit 2 together all the way across the
    row, so that 12 stitches remain.
4. Knit 6 rows in A, break off yarn and transfer the frill to
    a stitch holder.

Make several more pieces in this way, knitting either more
or fewer rows at step 4 in order to make the piece longer or
shorter as desired.

To attach the frilled sections to the base that you are
knitting, transfer one section to the working needle and
knit 12 rows in garter stitch. Then move another frilled
section to a spare double-pointed needle. Place this frill to
the back of the knitting, with the spare needle parallel to
the main working needle. Insert the other working needle
through both a stitch from the frill and the equivalent
stitch on the main needle and knit them off together.
Continue in this manner until all of the add-ons have been
incorporated into the knitting.

right

Sample showing five
add-on frills joined into
a garter-stitched piece.

Knitted-In Extensions

The frond-like extensions on *Spirit Dresses* (see chapter 10) are knitted by casting on and off the same number of stitches at various points along the row, rather than by making and then adding a separate length of edging.

These extensions can be made longer or shorter by casting on and off more or fewer stitches and more widely spaced or closely packed, as desired. You can knit extra rows between the cast on and cast-off rows of each frond. By casting on a large number of stitches on a circular knitting needle, it is possible to knit long lengths across the width of the needle with fronds incorporated into the knitting at regular intervals.

Try a short sample on two needles before making a length. First, cast on any number of stitches that can be divided by 3, plus 2 extra stitches to form the left-hand edges. Knit several rows until you reach the frond row. Work thus:

1. * Knit 3 stitches. To make the frond, slip the last stitch knitted back onto the left-hand needle. Cast on (for example) 5 stitches, then cast them off again. *
2. Repeat from * to * as required – until you have used all but 2 stitches in your row.
3. Knit the final 2 stitches of the row.

This is how you make the extension within the frond (step 1 above): *Do not count the stitch you have just transferred to the left needle as a new stitch.* To make the first new stitch, insert the right needle into this loop and pass the yarn around the needle as if to knit. Knit the stitch, drawing through the new loop and slipping it onto the left needle to form a new stitch. Repeat this operation until you have 5 new stitches on the left needle.

To cast off, knit the first 2 stitches of this group of 5 stitches. Draw the loop of the first stitch over the second stitch, leaving 1 stitch from this group of 5 stitches on the right needle. Knit the next stitch, and then draw the first stitch over the needle. One stitch of this group will remain on the right needle. Continue to work thus until all of the new 5 stitches have been cast back off. The stitch you slipped from right to left needle at the beginning of this sequence should now be on the right needle.

This sample (right) is worked over a large number of stitches with proportionally few rows, on 12mm (US size 17) circular knitting needles. The technique means that the extensions will hang vertically along the full width of the knitting. The circular needles are used in the same way as standard knitting needles, but allow for a greater number of stitches to be cast on than the latter.

below

Knitted-in 'frond' extension.

The sample above was knitted in Colinette Enigma (A) and 2 strands of Colinette Fandango (B). Colour A was first knitted into a slip-stitch tube on a chunky-gauge knitting machine, over 5 stitches on tension 7. To do the same in hand knitting, work on double-pointed needles thus: cast on 3 stitches (for example) from right to the left. Move these stitches back up the needle to the right, taking the working yarn to the back of the needle. Knit one row. Move these stitches back up the needle and continue in the same manner as required (see the slip-stitch tube knitted in Rowan Big Wool, E on page 10).

above

Sample collar.

Once the slip-stitch tube is complete, use it to cast on 30 stitches.
1. Knit 2 rows in A.
2. Using B, make extensions every 3rd stitch by using the technique described above – but this time make the cast-on/cast-off extensions 8 stitches deep.
3. Knit 1 more row in B.
4. Change to A and knit 1 row.
5. On the next row, knit 2 together followed by a make 1. Do this all the way along the row.
6. Knit 2 more rows in A.
7. Change to B and knit extensions 5 stitches deep every 3rd stitch.
8. Knit 1 row in B.

The sample opposite is an idea for a dramatic collar knitted on circular needles, this shaped swatch was decreased over the width of the row at regular intervals. Commencing with 48 stitches, the first row of multiple decreases was made thus: knit 2 stitches and knit the next 2 stitches together. Repeat this instruction across the row.

The sample below shows machine-knitted samples developing knit and turn (short-row) techniques with castings on and off, knitted on a standard-gauge machine in wire, sewing thread and fine glitter yarns. These examples show the links between hand knitting and machine knitting; all could if desired be knitted by hand, although the ultra-fine yarns would be time-consuming to knit in this way. You can make short-row knitting like this on the most basic of machines, where the technique is referred to as holding position or partial knitting.

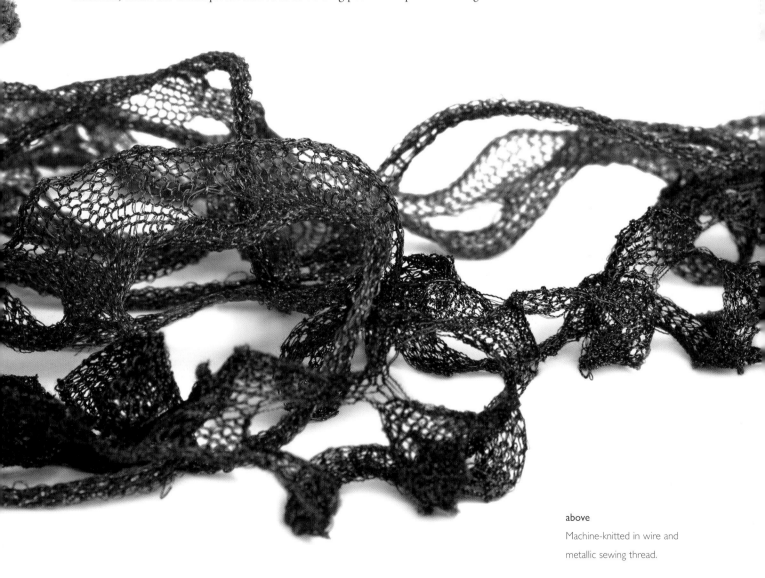

above

Machine-knitted in wire and metallic sewing thread.

5 Knitting with Beads

You can incorporate beads and bead-like objects into a piece of work during the knitting process to create added texture, outline a clearly defined design, or act as focal points within the knitting. By 'bead' I mean any suitable item that is drilled for stringing or threading. This includes conventional manufactured beads and handmade beads but also encompasses found and recycled objects, and industrial hardware such as brass nuts, washers, grommets and rings.

Your choice of knitting medium for working with beads could be anything from fine waxed linen thread to transparent fishing line or marine rope – it will all depend upon the scale and context of the work. Most of the sampling in this chapter was inspired by the natural world: seashells, sea urchins, starfish and frill-neck lizards, for example, but suits of armour were also contributory sources.

right

Combining yarns or threads of different weights with beads produces a wonderfully textural finished effect.

About Beads

Commercially produced beads are available in any number of different materials, shapes and sizes. Materials include glass, plastic, wood, metal, porcelain, resin and crystal. Beads can be opaque, translucent, metallic, enamelled, transparent or solid colours. The sample opposite shows three of the glass beads available. These are fire-polished glass beads, which are heated to a high temperature to give them a clean glossy surface, beads coloured with AB (an iridescent coating) and metallic beads. See those at GJ Beads, for example (www.gjbeads.co.uk).

As already mentioned, almost anything that has a hole, or can receive a drilled hole, can be used as a bead: washers, hexagonal nuts, grommets, curtain rings, plastic rings, and also discs and tubes of any kind with holes, plastic tubing or bottle tops cut down to form beads, for example (see below). You can also drill holes in naturally occurring materials such as shells, stones, slices of cork, discs of thin wood, lengths of cane (with holes drilled into them) or feathers. Consider using buttons (with or without shanks), sequins or charms, or make handmade beads from, for example, rolled, painted and varnished paper, wrapped and burnt Tyvek, or distressed metals (see chapter 9 for more on this).

right

Sampler incorporating fire-polished beads (top), iridescent beads (centre) and metallic beads (bottom). The sampler is worked in wire.

below

Washers make an unusual alternative to beads but note that they must be used with strong yarn because they are heavy.

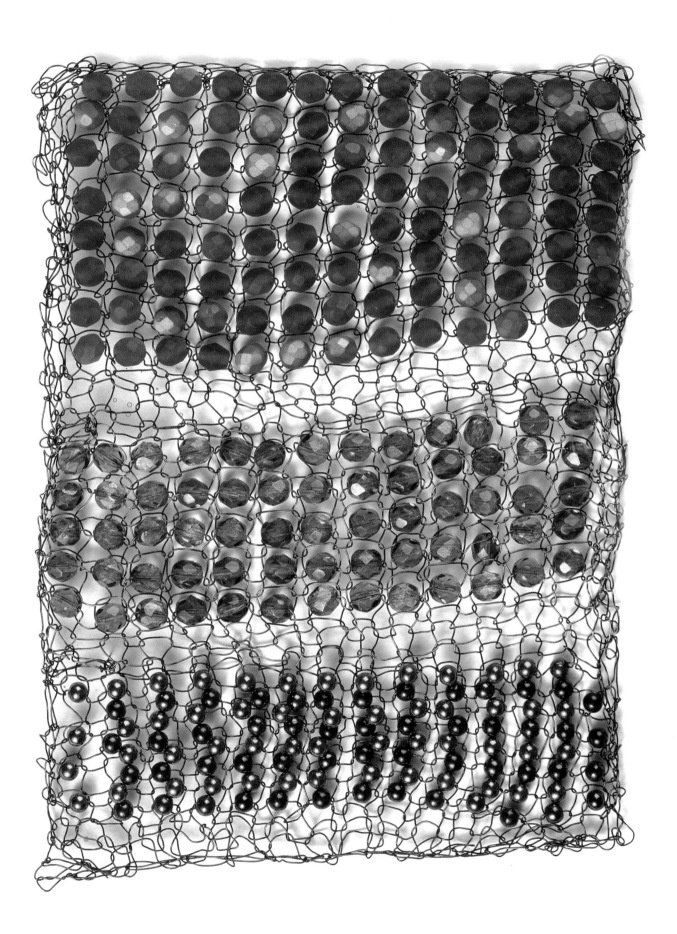

Knitting Techniques

There are three main techniques for knitting with beads, irrespective of choice of stitch patterns and knitting yarns and fibres, and each technique has its own merits. Designed to ensure that the beads move with the knitting rather than simply sitting on top of the surface (as would be the case if they were stitched on), these techniques offer ways of integrating knitting and beads, both structurally and visually.

In the first method the beads are pre-strung onto a knitting medium ready for knitting. Once knitted, the beads sit in between the stitches and are generally visible from the front of the knitting only. The second technique also involves knitting with pre-strung beads, but now the bead is drawn through the stitch as the knitting progresses. The handle of the fabric is much more fluid when knitted this way. The third method uses a totally different approach in which beads are inserted into the knitting on a stitch-by-stitch basis. The loop of the stitch is drawn through the hole of the bead using a small crochet hook, or a needle and thread. The beads are visible from both sides of the knitting. Additional techniques might include making closed pockets in the same manner as the tubular knitted fabrics (see page 38) to contain the beads: this is particularly useful for incorporating large objects.

In all of the methods sampled below the beads can either be knitted-in after every stitch or spaced out after every second, third (or more) stitch across the row, depending upon the type of design you intend to make. Several rows can be knitted-in between beading rows, or beads can be incorporated on every row, although the latter will make the work very heavy and is best suited to small beads or for making non-functional gallery pieces.

Before embarking on a large-scale bead-knitting project, you should indeed consider the impact of the added weight of the beads on the finished piece – and also the strength of the carrier thread. Calculate roughly how many beads might be needed, then weigh a known number, for example ten, and multiply it to determine the weight of the finished piece (not forgetting your estimated weight of the yarn and other materials). If weight is a problem you could consider deceiving the eye by using hand painted and varnished paper beads in place of heavy glass or ceramic beads.

Threading Beads onto the Knitting Medium

In two of the bead-knitting techniques described, beads are threaded onto the knitting medium before starting to knit. In both cases, the beads you thread last will be the first to be knitted.

Beads can be purchased loose or pre-strung onto a temporary thread ready for transferring to the knitting medium of your choice. Remember that pre-strung beads, though quick to work, restrict your choice of bead to a single colour and type. To transfer pre-strung beads from a bought-in hank to your knitting medium, simply tie the end of the temporary thread they come on to a loop made in the knitting medium, then slide the beads carefully from one to the other.

To string up loose beads, first empty the beads into a shallow dish. Cut approximately 20cm (8in) of strong sewing thread. Insert both cut ends of the thread into a sewing needle to make a loop (before you do this, check that the eye of the needle will go through the holes in the beads). Pass the knitting yarn through this loop of thread to create a second, connected loop. Scoop up beads with the needle, and thread them in the order required for pattern, transferring beads from the temporary loop of thread to the doubled over main yarn as you go.

Larger beads, such as buttons, can be picked up with a crochet hook and transferred to the knitting medium, or simply incorporated as the knitting progresses (see method 3).

Method 1

This method is knitted with pre-strung beads that sit between the stitches. Sections A–D of this sample (right) show different ways of incorporating the beads, for example from the front or the back of the knitting, and on knit or purl facing rows.

If possible, choose a needle size slightly smaller than normal to knit, so that the stitches are close together – this will help keep the beads to the front side of the work. There is a danger of stitches migrating to the back of the work with this method if you knit on too loose a tension. The slip-stitch version closes gaps in the knitting and reduces the possibilities of this happening.

These examples are knitted on 3mm (US size 2½) metal needles in 0.315mm enamelled copper wire (from the Scientific Wire Company). The beads were pre-threaded for sections A to E, while sections F and G incorporated them into the knitting as the work progressed. For each method below, cast on an odd number of stitches plus two extra edge stitches at both ends, for example 17 stitches in total.

right

Sample of beaded

knitting techniques.

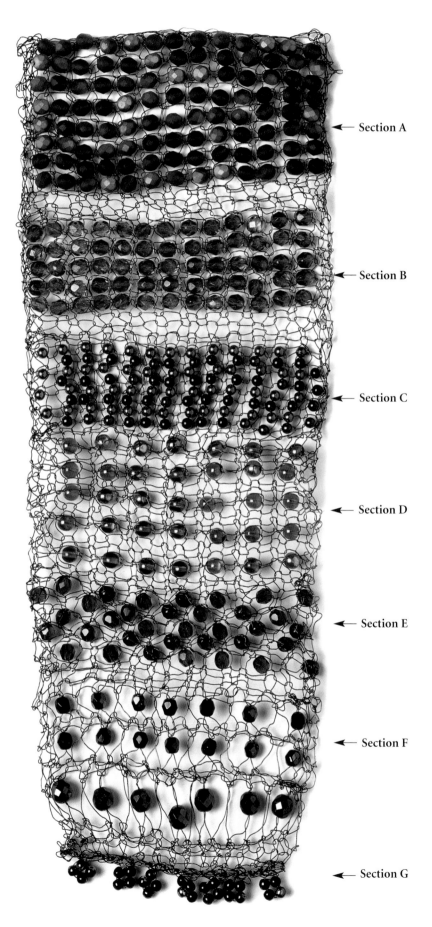

← Section A

← Section B

← Section C

← Section D

← Section E

← Section F

← Section G

Section A is knitted using knit for all rows. The beads are added after every stitch on the wrong side row thus:

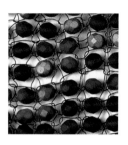

> **Row 1:** Knit all stitches.
> **Row 2:** Knit 2, * move the bead up the yarn or wire, close to the knitting on the side facing *away* from you (this side will be the front of the work). Hold the bead firmly in place and knit the next stitch. *. Repeat from * to * until 2 stitches remain. Knit 2.

Section B the beads are added in from the front on purl stitches.

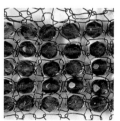

> **Row 1:** Knit 2, * move the bead up the yarn or wire close to the knitting on the side facing you. Hold the bead firmly in place and purl the next stitch. *. Repeat from * to * until 2 stitches remain. Knit 2.
> **Row 2:** Knit or purl all stitches, keeping the edge stitches as knit stitches throughout.

Section C is beaded on every row and before every stitch with 4mm (⅙in) beads.

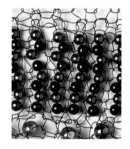

> **Row 1:** Knit 2, * move the bead up the yarn or wire close to the knitting on the side facing you. Hold the bead firmly in place and purl the next stitch. *. Repeat from * to * until 2 stitches remain. Knit 2.
> **Row 2:** Knit 2, * move the bead up the yarn or wire close to the knitting on the side facing away from you (which is the front of the work). Hold the bead firmly in place and knit the next stitch. *. Repeat from * to * until 2 stitches remain. Knit 2. Repeat these two rows throughout.

Section D incorporates slipped stitches after the 6mm (¼in) Amethyst AB glass beads (from GJ Beads) are moved into position on the knit facing row thus:

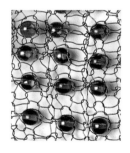

> **Row 1:** Knit 2, * yarn forward, move bead into position on the right side, slip the next stitch knit-wise, yarn to back of work, knit 1 *. Repeat from * to * until 1 stitch remains. Knit 1.
> **Row 2:** Knit 2, purl 13 and knit 2.
> **Row 3:** Knit all stitches.
> **Row 4:** Repeat row 2.

Note that rows 3 and 4 are optional, depending upon the size of the beads. It is also possible to move more than one bead into the forward position, at the same time slipping the corresponding number of stitches before working the next knit stitch.

Method 2

In this method the beads are drawn through the stitch as the knitting progresses. Twisted stocking stitch is often used with this technique, so those beads sit vertically in the more closely beaded patterns. However, note that a bias can occur in these twisted stocking stitch patterns.

To knit twisted stocking stitch you need to knit into the *back* of the loop instead of the normal method, where you would knit into the front of the loop. At the same time, bring the bead up close to the left-hand needle, and push it through the stitch loop as you knit the stitch off, ensuring that it sits to the front of the work.

Section E is knitted with pre-threaded 6mm (¼in) faceted amethyst beads (from GJ Beads) on every other stitch and on every other row, using twisted knit stitches. On every alternate beading row, the position of the beads is staggered one bead to the left. Knit one or more rows between each beading row. Small beads can be knitted into every stitch for closely packed patterns.

Method 3

In this method the beads are inserted into the knitting on a stitch-by-stitch basis. The loop of the knitted stitch is drawn through the hole of the bead, and then knitted off, so that the individual beads sit on the stitch itself rather than between the stitches (as happens in the previous method). A similar working method is used in machine knitting. The stitch will need to be long enough to go through the hole of the bead, and with enough slack so you can insert the point of the knitting needle into it to make the next stitch. Beads can be added over a standard length stitch, elongated stitches and made stitches (using the yarn-over method). Make the elongated stitches or made stitch on the row *prior* to knitting in the beads.

Elongated stitches and made stitches have advantages over a standard-length stitch. The extra length of these stitches allows you to incorporate columns of beads, one on top of the other, or larger beads into the knitting. You can also knit with industrial-scale or unusual materials (see pages 58 and 70).

To add the bead using this method, work as follows:

1. Knit to the point in the work where you want to incorporate the bead.
2. Insert a small metal crochet hook through the hole in the bead, or use a needle and strong thread to transfer the bead to the stitch loop.
3. Remove the next stitch from the left-hand needle with the hook or the needle.
4. Pull this stitch through the hole in the bead with either the crochet hook or needle and thread.
5. Finally, replace the stitch onto the working needle prior to knitting or purling it off.

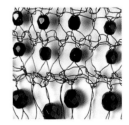

Section F is produced by first knitting one row of elongated stitches – in this example, a double-throw stitch was sufficiently long to accommodate the 6mm (¼in) facetted carnival blue iris beads. On the next row, add beads over every alternate stitch. Complete the pattern sequence with a knit row of standard-length stitches. Repeat this sequence twice. Repeat once more with triple-throw elongated stitches to accommodate 8mm (⅜in) facetted beads. Both types of bead in this example were from GJ Beads.

Section G features beaded swags on a carrier thread (B) that is separate to the main knitting medium (A). The small beads were threaded up on a second length of wire. The first two stitches of the row were knitted in A plus B. The next two stitches were knitted in A, while B plus 4 beads made a separate loop. Knit the next two stitches in A plus B. Continue working in this manner across the width of the row.

The sample below shows enamelled copper wire and glass beads knitted in the round, a development of working method 3. See chapter 7 for advanced techniques for knitting in the round.

Working from Graphs

To string up a bead pattern from a graph such as that shown in this diagram (opposite), you need to work in reverse order, remembering to go back to the beginning of each line of the graph when knitting beads on every alternate row. For beading on every row, thread one row following the graph from left to right and the next row from the right to the left.

below

Beaded knitting in the round.

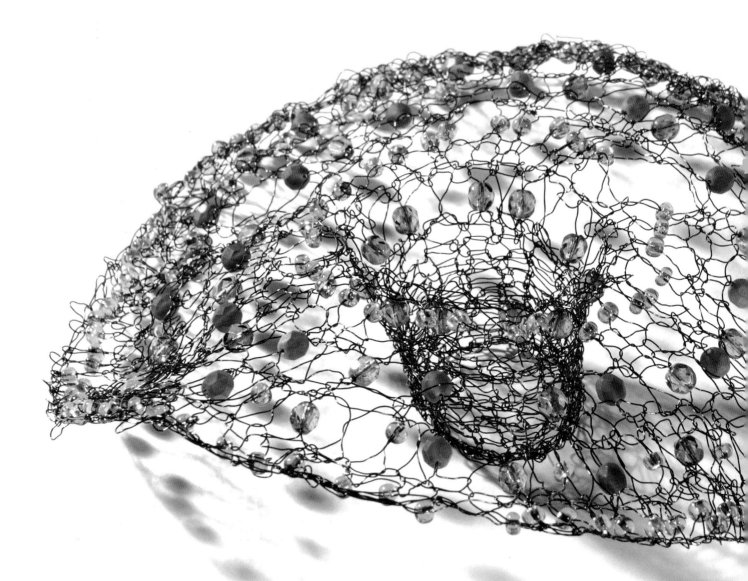

right

Bead knitting graph.

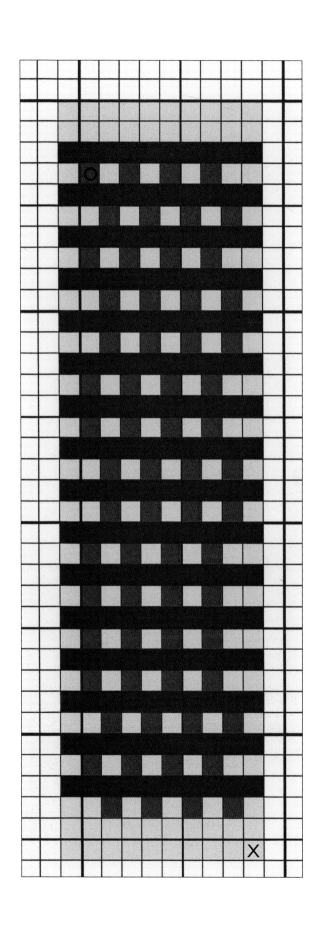

■ beads colour B
■ beads colour A
□ knit stitches
■ purl stitches
O start threading beads here
  before you start to knit
X start knitting here

Design Decisions

Your choice of beads, knitting technique and materials to knit with, and how each relates to the other, are of paramount importance when making design decisions. Any combinations of fibres and materials can be used to good effect, depending upon the desired outcome.

Compare, for example, how each of the different bead-knitting methods described above affects the handle of the knitting, particularly when it comes to heavily beaded knitting. Method 2 produces a more fluid fabric, whereas with method 1 the knitting is stiffer in handle.

Consider also the role of the knitting medium. In some examples of beaded knitting the knitting functions as an almost invisible carrier for whatever objects are incorporated into it, whereas in other examples knitting and beads are both highly visible, and work together to create exciting textures and patterns. Decide whether you want the colour of the knitting medium to match the beads, or to create a definite contrast. This is particularly important if you choose to knit with transparent beads, since the knitting medium will be visible.

Having mastered the basics of bead knitting, the next step is to experiment freely with different knitting materials and beads, and various combinations of techniques. Refer to your personal sketchbooks for inspiration on colour, texture and pattern. These open-ended experiments will lead to a more focused and refined approach to sampling, so connecting your workshop practice with concept development and finished pieces.

The samples below demonstrate the versatility of bead-knitting techniques, and the range of work it is possible to create. Each example has a very different character due to a unique combination of inspiration, knitting medium, beads and technique. Some are at the experimental stage while others are more fully developed.

The samples shown here (right and opposite) are part of a group of small, experimental pieces knitted in thick and thin yarns, incorporating shells, mother of pearl beads and buttons, as well as off-the-shelf pillar beads. The beads are worked in using combinations of garter stitch, stocking stitch, slip-stitch and developing method 1. The use of related colours and surface tie this group together visually.

above left
Beads knitted in using a variety of stitches, using Colinette Enigma and linen thread.

above right
Spool-knitted sample.

In the samples shown left the carrier yarn for the strung beads is a strong linen thread (from Empress Mills). The knitting between the beading rows is worked in Colinette Enigma yarn – the subtle blends of colour complement the beads and shells, and contrast well with the smoother linen thread that carries the beads.

The neckpieces (shown on the following page) are based on traditional household braids, and inspired by the outer surfaces of starfish and other undersea creatures. This was further developed into *Relics*, an experimental textile art piece knitted in Tyvek and wire, incorporating heat-treated handmade beads (see page 116).

In the shaping techniques here, functional made stitches (yarn forward method) are used as a way of producing the triangular edge-shapes. The bead-knitting techniques are a development of method 3, combining elongated stitches, made eyelets and standard-length knit stitches. See page 97 for more detailed instructions on sideways-knitted shaped edgings.

below

Here the colours of the yarn and thread bring out certain colours in the pearl beads for a rich harmonizing effect.

right

A more fluid structure
than the other examples;
the glass beads move with
the knitting when in wear.
In this example the beads
are incorporated over
softer yarns (Rowan
Shimmer and Noro Ganpi
Abaka tape).

below

Neckpiece knitted in
enamelled wires and
transparent display line with
amethyst beads.

below
Collar in wire and
Rowan Shimmer, with
recycled beads.

Cable, Washers and Outsize Glass Beads

The examples here show a collection of big, architectural braids and modern bags, in complete contrast to the previous examples. They were knitted on 15mm (US size 19) plastic knitting needles using marine rope and single-core electrical cable, adorned with brass and zinc washers, hexagonal nuts, metal curtain runners and outsize glass beads. Here, the aim was to create a hard-edged industrial look, inspired by protective suits of armour.

The bag shown above is knitted in black single core electrical cable, with added-in copper washers. It is an example of contemporary bag design with associated experimental samples shown below (see also page 58).

above

Contemporary bag knitted in marine rope, with copper washers and plastic beads.

below

Industrial beads.

Paper Beads, Painted Paper and Wire

The piece shown above is part of a group of experimental surfaces in which I explored ways of combining handmade paper beads with knitting in painted paper yarns. The result was expressive surfaces where each individual component is like a brushstroke on a painting.

A further development can be seen in chapter 9, where handmade and Tyvek beads have been knitted into painted and distressed Tyvek and enamelled copper wire. This example was part of a collection of textile art works inspired by the notion of 'relics'.

Various stitch patterns and structures offer wide scope for the adventurous artist to explore and sample, from simple garter-stitch, stocking-stitch and slip-stitch designs through to multicoloured patterned knitting and intarsia (inlaid) work, elongated stitches and openwork knitting techniques. Shaping techniques such as short-row knitting and made stitches can be exploited to great effect, with beads emphasizing directional changes within the piece.

above

Wire and paper yarn knitting with beads made from rolled paper strips.

6 Spool and Frame Knitting Techniques

Influenced by basketry structures and vessel-like containers, this chapter considers how to create three-dimensional forms in the round as an integral part of the knitting process, using simple knitting frames and spools – knitting without needles. Sometimes referred to as rake knitting, ring knitting, corking or French knitting, the most familiar version of the technique is the knitting spool used by children to make continuous lengths of tubular knitting.

The current revival in hand knitting has seen a wide range of spools and frames become more readily available (see page 12). These include round wooden spools with four or more wooden pegs, and straight wooden frames with pegs set in on each of the long sides of a centre slit. Both straight fabrics and tubular knitting are possible on the latter.

As a working method, spool knitting is closer to machine knitting than hand knitting. Indeed, the tools and equipment involved could be considered a primitive version of the domestic knitting machine. Spool knitting is a technique that is simple to use, immediate and visual. It offers the creative knitter the chance to work and think directly in three dimensions, without resorting to complex technologies and expensive equipment.

In this chapter I shall focus on creating shaped, seamless tubular forms in a range of hard and soft materials, using standard knitting techniques such as knit and purl stitches in various combinations, slip stitch, two-colours stranded knitting, short-row knitting, and openwork stitch patterns.

The Basics

In spool knitting the wool is looped around four nails or staples set in the top of a wooden cotton reel. After two such windings have been made, the bottom row of loops are lifted over the top row with a metal pick or crochet hook. The main challenge faced by the spool knitter comes from the relatively limited opportunities to alter the gauge of the knitting, in comparison with working on standard needles. This is because the spacing and size of the pegs and the thickness of the yarns dictate the gauge of the knitting.

right

Detail of the sample
shown on page 75.

Casting On

First, pull the end of yarn down the centre of the bobbin, then start winding the yarn loosely around each of the pegs from the back to the front in a clockwise direction. Bring the yarn from the back of the last wrapped peg to the front of the first wrapped peg. Holding the bobbin in your left hand and the pick (a double-pointed knitting needle or crochet hook, for example) in your right, pull the bottom loop of yarn over the top row of yarn. Pull the loose end of yarn downward to secure this first stitch.

Stitches

There are two methods of working a **knit stitch** in spool knitting; a flat wrap and an E wrap. The former makes a tighter stitch, the latter a larger stitch.

To knit a larger stitch, wrap the working yarn around the peg from back to the front of the pegs (as for casting on). For a tighter stitch, lay the yarn around the outside of the pegs without winding, then lift the stitch already on the peg over the winding from the outside over to the inside to create a new stitch.

If every stitch on every round is worked as a knit stitch (that is, with the knot of the stitch always facing away from the knitter), the result will be the same as working stocking stitch – one row knit, followed by one row purl, on two needles.

It is possible to knit purl stitches on round spools with a little bit of ingenuity. Remember that the main difference to a knit stitch is that the knot of the purl stitch faces the knitter, and the smooth side faces into the spool.

To make a **purl stitch** on a circular spool, lay the working thread around the outside of the next peg, making sure that it is situated *below* the loop of the stitch already on the peg. Using the pick, reach down through the loop of the existing stitch and draw a new loop up through the old stitch. Pull the new stitch up until the old stitch comes off to the inside of the spool. Now slip the new stitch onto the empty peg.

As in conventional knitting, a **slip stitch** simply means a stitch that has been transferred to the working needle without knitting or purling it. For single-colour slip-stitch patterns in spool knitting the yarn is stranded across the back of the stitch to be slipped (instead of lifting the stitch over it) so that it is available to the next peg, where it can be used to work the next knit or purl stitch (or another slip stitch, if appropriate).

Casting Off

To cast off, first place the working end of yarn behind the next peg to be knitted. Transfer the last stitch you have knitted to this next peg. There will now be two loops on this peg. Bring the lower loop on the peg over the upper loop. Pull the knitting down tightly. Continue in this manner until 1 stitch remains. Cut the yarn, leaving a long end to pull through the remaining loop. To make a looser cast-off, knit each loop one or more times before transferring it to the next peg for casting off as described above.

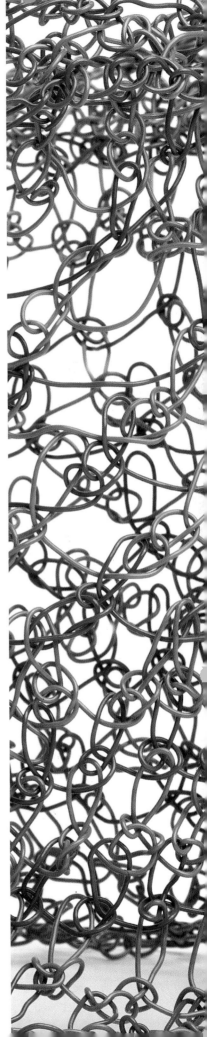

right

Detail of sample shown
on page 81.

Solid Stitch Patterns

This first group of samples was worked in easy-to-knit smooth big wool on a 24-peg frame, so that the stitch patterns were clearly defined. To transform these soft and flexible tubes into free-standing forms, explore a variety of different materials, as shown below.

The eight sections in the sample below are each 5 rows deep worked on a 24-peg frame. Notice the difference to the profile of the tube for each of the patterns. This undulating effect can be exaggerated with considered placement of, for example, rigid and stretchy stitch patterns.

Sections:

1. Knit-facing stocking stitch.
2. Purl-facing stocking stitch.
3. Knit 3 purl 3 rib.
4. Two-colour pattern knitting (see opposite).
5. Textured pattern in knit and purl stitches (see opposite).
6. Slip stitch pattern over two rounds: round one slip 2, knit 1 and round two knit 2, slip 1.
7. Knit-facing stocking stitch.
8. Purl-facing stocking stitch.

Knitting on a spool involves thinking in rounds rather than rows. In order to keep track, mark the beginning of the first round with a tie-in thread.

As already mentioned, knit-facing **stocking stitch** is all rounds knit, purl facing stocking stitch all rounds purl. To work **garter stitch** in circular knitting, knit 1 round, purl 1 round. Repeat these instructions as many times as required.

For single-colour **slip-stitch** patterns, two rounds of knitting are made where the slip stitches on the previous round are knitted, and the knit stitches from the previous round slipped. For example * knit 2, slip 1* repeat from * to * to end of round. Next round is *slip 2, knit 1 * repeat from * to * to the end of the round. Change colours every 2 rounds, or continue to knit in the same colour throughout.

below

Solid stitch patterns knitted in the round.

Two-colour patterns are simple geometric patterns knitted with two colours in a row, these are essentially a slip-stitch technique whereby selected pegs are knitted in colour A, and the remaining pegs in colour B. The colour not being knitted is stranded across the back of the work on the inside of the spool, until it is next required.

Slip-stitch knitting, whether in one or more colours, has a firm, non-stretchy handle compared with stocking stitch or rib knitting and works well in free-standing pieces.

Knit and purl patterns fall into two broad types. Rib structures are very elastic patterns in which knit and purl stitches alternate (as in knit 2, purl 2 rib) and all of the knit stitches are always knitted on the following rounds while the purl stitches are always purled. Textured patterns combine knit and purl patterns that are offset from each other on following rounds. This creates a firm-handling fabric, less stretchy than ribs.

Openwork Stitch Patterns

Openwork includes **eyelets**, ladders and patterns created from twice-knit stitches. To create eyelets in the round, manually transfer a stitch from one peg to the next adjacent peg stitch, leaving one empty peg followed by a peg with two stitches, and so creating a gap in the knitting. Lift the bottom loop over the top loop, or knit both stitches off together on the next round (this is similar to the manual transfer of stitches on the domestic knitting machine).

To create an openwork **ladder** effect, transfer a stitch from one peg to the next adjacent peg. You can either continue to knit on this reduced number of stitches, or rewind the empty pegs on the next or following rounds. Try different spacing between pegs with working stitches and the empty pegs. Knitting on different numbers of stitches within the same piece works as a shaping device, by increasing and decreasing the diameter of the tube you are creating.

Twice-knitted stitch technique allows you to create sturdy, structurally stable, openwork hollow forms on a relatively large scale. To knit this stitch, first knit one stitch then, keeping to the same peg, knit another stitch over the top of the first stitch. Additional stitches can be worked, which are knitted in two colours of connecting cable with two and three stitches each peg on some rounds and three or five stitches on each peg on other rounds.

below

Openwork stitch patterns knitted in the round.

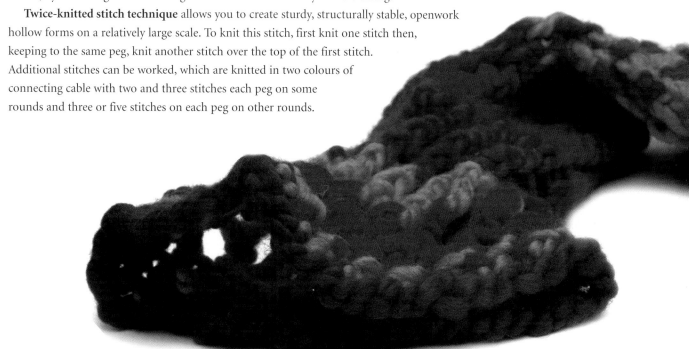

Shaping Techniques

Working between different stitch patterns is one method of altering the shape of the tube without the need to increase or decrease the number of working stitches – for example by knitting different sections of plain knitting, garter stitch, slip stitch and rib.

Other shaping methods include combining empty pegs with pegs that contain working stitches. Cast on over every other peg (or every 3rd peg, for instance) and knit several rounds. Knit 1 peg, then cast on over the empty peg to increase the width of the knitting. You can do this over one full round or stagger the cast-on over several rounds to create interesting, asymmetrical shapes.

Try knitting alternating rounds with thick and thin materials. This is a good way both to create shape and to vary the density of the knitting. Try the same process using hard and soft fibres and see what effects you can achieve.

You can also work between spools with different numbers of pegs to create wide and narrow shapes. To do this, you will need to take the knitting off the larger sized spool and replace the stitches onto a smaller size spool, doubling up stitches where necessary. To make the process of moving the stitches over a bit easier you could first knit a few rounds in scrap yarn so that the last row of the actual knitting doesn't come unravelled during the transfer process, or you can use a twin pin to remove and replace the stitches.

Further Techniques

Here are some more complex techniques for spool knitting. The next chapter provides further advanced techniques, while chapter 4 provides more information on the short-row technique and chapter 9 has more on vertical and horizontal slits.

To create **vertical slits** in tubular forms, work back and forth on 8 stitches for 13 rows (for example). Break off the yarn and move on to the next group of 8 stitches, repeating the process in the same or different yarn. You can use this technique to create spiralling tubes with offset vertical slits – to do this, the number of stitches between each slit should not divide evenly into the number of stitches cast on.

Shaping in short-round knitting can also create interesting effects. Knit back and forth in rows, on fewer and fewer stitches, to form a wedge shape. For example, if the round consists of 24 stitches (pegs) you could knit 22 stitches and turn and knit back in the opposite direction for 20 stitches, turn and knit 18 stitches, turn and knit 16 stitches, and so on until you are left with just 2 stitches to knit. Now reverse the process: knit 4 stitches and turn, knit 6 stitches and turn, knit 8 stitches and turn, until you are knitting all 24 stitches.

Straight Knitting Frames

You can use a straight knitting frame to make ribbed and tubular fabrics. A straight frame is rectangular in shape with pegs around the long edges.

To work a closed cast-on, make a slip-knot over the first peg on the back left of the frame. Wind the yarn across the opening and around the first peg on the front of the frame clockwise, back crosswise over the opening to the next peg on the back anti-clockwise, and so on across the frame (see diagram, right).

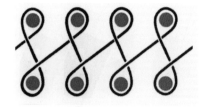

Knitting a Flat Fabric

To knit a simple knit 1 purl 1 rib, first cast on (as above). On the next row, wind the yarn between the back and front pegs (see diagram, right) all the way along the frame. Knit the bottom loop off over the top loop on the peg, working your way around the frame.

You can alter how you wind the pegs, for example winding two pegs on the front of the frame followed by two pegs on the back of the frame. You can also alternate between ribbed and tubular fabric, as shown below.

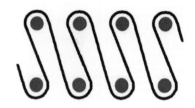

left

Ribbed and turbular structure knitted on a straight peg frame.

Moving On

These three small collections show sampling at different points of the development process. I hope they will provide you with ideas for your own explorations.

Here are some potential ideas for cuffs, bracelets and small bags, made as an exploration of different knitting mediums to create free-standing solid forms. The examples are knitted in off-the-shelf lightweight, modern tape yarn, custom-made cordage from strips of fabric, and tutu net with beading elastic.

The samples opposite are a group of resolved pieces ready for further development into their final forms. Knitting in single-core connecting cable and Rowan Big Wool, I felted the latter to emphasize both the solid and openwork stitch patterns and the visual contrast between the softness of the natural fibres and hard man-made materials. I used colour to link these last two aspects together.

To close the open ends of this kind of work, transfer half the stitches each to a standard knitting needle and cast the stitches off together (picking up one from each needle at the same time) with a third needle (see page 34 for how to do this). Alternatively, you can cast on over a straight frame and knit a closed stitch pattern for the bottom section, moving on to circular knitting for the uppermost section. You can always transfer the work from the straight frame onto a circular spool that has a smaller number of pegs.

below

Ideas for cuffs, bracelets and small bags.

opposite

Ideas for pocket bags in felted wool and connecting cable.

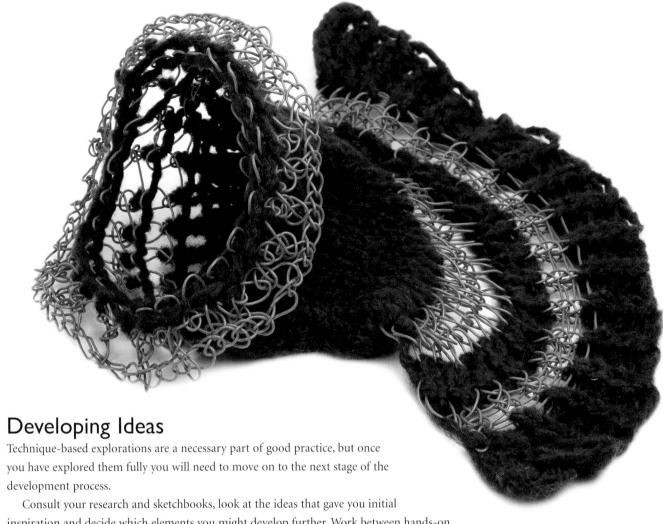

Developing Ideas

Technique-based explorations are a necessary part of good practice, but once
you have explored them fully you will need to move on to the next stage of the
development process.

Consult your research and sketchbooks, look at the ideas that gave you initial
inspiration and decide which elements you might develop further. Work between hands-on
sampling and sketchbooks, observing how different mediums affect the look and the handle
of the knitting. Then select and refine those samples that best express your ideas visually.

The problem in this group (below and opposite) was how to knit tubular forms that would keep their shape, and also how to emphasize the contrast between negative space and positive linear patterns, making references to basketry construction techniques. One way of doing this was by knitting in two-colour slip stitch.

The second challenge was to create openwork forms that didn't collapse under their own weight of connecting cable. I solved this by knitting the openwork sections with twice- and three-times-knitted stitches, combined with the solidity of slip stitch patterns (see page 75 for detailed instructions on these kinds of knit stitches.) The sample shown opposite is knitted completely in interlocking stitches, and is surprisingly rigid.

To knit the standing form of the sample opposite proceed as follows:

1. Knit a section 8 rounds deep on all 24 pegs.
2. The middle section is 5 rows deep and is knitted on 12 pegs only. To reduce the stitches, transfer every alternate stitch to the adjacent peg as described above.
3. Leaving one stitch on the peg, continue to knit 2 more stitches above this stitch (blue round).
4. Knit a further 5 rounds.

On the next orange round, knit the empty pegs to fill in the gaps, as follows:

5. Wrap the wire around the peg twice and make 1 stitch.
6. Now knit 2 more stitches above this stitch (3 stitches in all).
7. Knit 8 rounds with 2 stitches on each peg on the blue rounds and 3 stitches on each peg on the orange rounds.
8. Cast off loosely.

below

Three openwork forms.

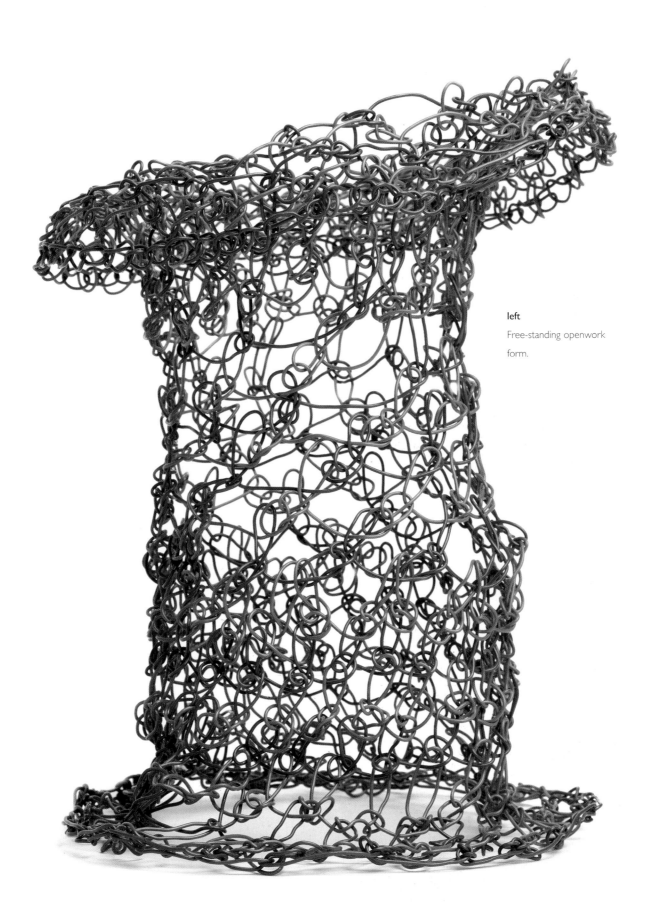

left

Free-standing openwork
form.

7 Advanced Techniques for Knitting in Rounds

Knitting constructed in the round can be flat and two dimensional, or a seamless three-dimensional tube. While chapter 6 covered spool-knitting techniques through simply constructed 3-dimensional forms, this chapter focuses on advanced circular knitting techniques as a means of creating free-standing constructions inspired by tree forms and growth patterns. Before moving onto the more advanced shaping techniques required for this, an understanding of how to knit flat shapes (see below) is necessary.

Two-Dimensional Shapes

I use 'shape' here to refer to that which is two-dimensional – having height and width but not depth. Examples of two-dimensional geometric shapes include circles, squares, triangles, hexagons and diamonds. The first group of samples investigates the mechanics of knitting these shapes in the round.

The final shape of the work is dictated by the process of making regular structural increases and decreases that are incorporated as the knitting progresses and either increase outwards from the centre or decrease inwards from the outside edge, depending on where they are placed in relation to each other. Structural increases and decreases can either be visible (for example, increasing by bringing the yarn forward before a knit stitch) or discreet (for example, increasing by knitting into both the front and back of a stitch).

Double-pointed needles and circular knitting needles are used for knitting in rounds when you want a flat surface such as a disc, hexagon or square shape. Commence the work on short sets of double-pointed needles, transferring the knitting to a circular needle once you have enough stitches to go around the length of the twin pin – or you can continue on longer double-pointed needles.

An equal division of stitches over four or five double-pointed needles is a good way to knit a square or pentagon, as the group of stitches on each needle each corresponds to one side of the shape. On circular needles you will need to use stitch markers to mark your place in the knitting where necessary. See right for examples of knitting in recycled telephone wire on Pony brand double-pointed needles set up for square and pentagon shapes. Also shown is a circular shape knitted in an openwork stitch pattern in 0.315mm ivory enamelled copper wire (from Scientific Wire Company) on Addi brand circular knitting needles.

Before commencing a major piece of work you should knit a tension swatch (see page 28) in the yarns and needles intended for the finished piece. From this you can calculate the ratio of stitches to rows and the tension necessary to guarantee a flat fabric.

right

Knitting squares, pentangles and circles in the round.

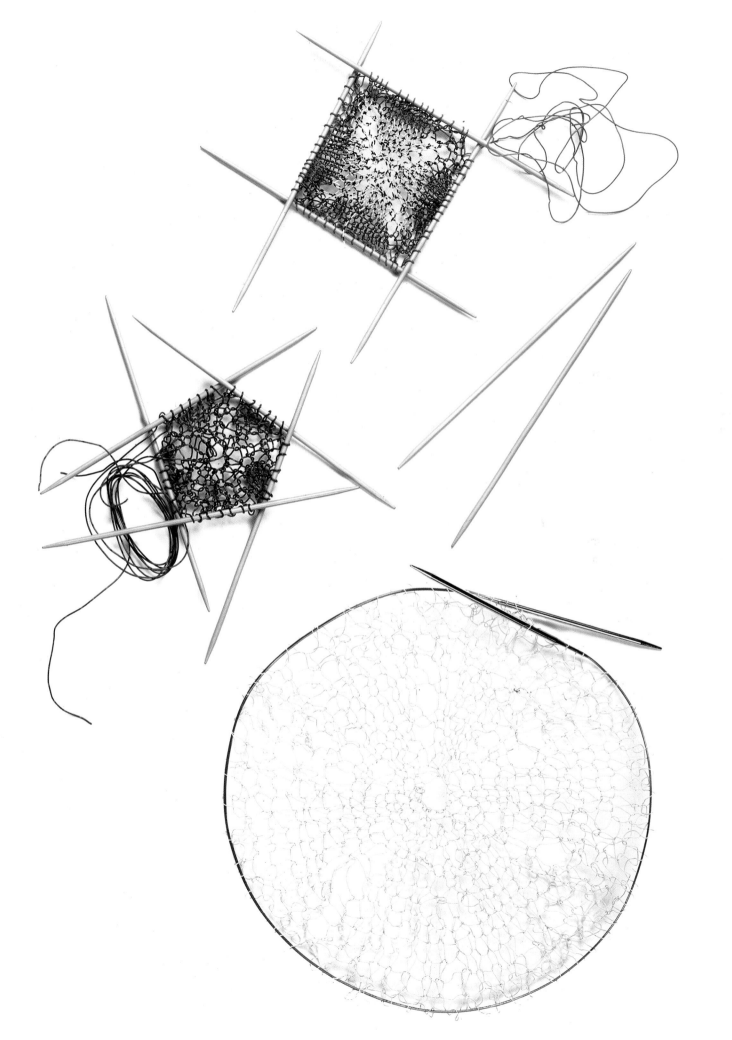

The following examples give some general guidance on how to knit flat shapes in the round.

Square

You will need five short double-pointed needles, four to hold the knitting and one as the working needle. The stitches are divided into four equal sections, and one group of stitches equals one side of the square. You can either work from the outside towards the inside, decreasing the stitches at regular intervals, or commence at the centre and increase outwards. Knitted in ribbon on 6mm (US size 10) double-pointed needles, the sample below was worked from the centre to the outside edge, using invisible increases.

Method:

1. Cast on 8 stitches on 1 double-pointed needle, or make a crochet chain of 8 loops.
2. Divide these stitches (loops) evenly between 4 double-pointed needles, 2 stitches per needle.
3. Using the 5th needle, commence knitting round 1. As each needle becomes free you use this as the new working needle. Knit all 8 stitches in this manner.
4. On the next round * make 1 stitch by bringing the yarn forward before knitting the next stitch, or knit once into the front of the stitch and once into the back of the same stitch *. Repeat from * to * 8 times in all. You now have 16 stitches (4 on each double-pointed needle). Knit 1 round.

The next 2 rounds form the pattern:

Round one: * make 1, knit 3, make 1, knit 1, *. Repeat from * to * 4 times in all.
Round two: knit or purl all stitches.

Repeat these 2 rows throughout, except that on the increase row increase the stitches on each needle by a factor of 2, for example * make 1, knit 5 (or 7, 9, 11), make 1, knit 1 *.

Continue expanding the number of stitches as described above until you reach the required size. Change colours for stripe effects, and add a few rows of purl-facing stitches for textural interest.

To knit a **rectangular shape** similar to that shown above cast on over 4 needles as follows: 6, 2, 6 and 2 stitches. Knit as above, expanding outwards in a similar manner to the square. In this example the final round was 20, 16, 20 and 16 stitches.

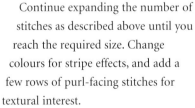

above
Rectangle shape knitted from the centre to the outer edges.

left
Square shape knitted from the centre outwards.

Pentagon

A five-sided geometric shape knitted with 6 double-pointed needles (5 needles to hold the stitches and one working needle).

Method:

1. To knit from the centre to the outside edge, cast on 10 stitches on 1 double-pointed needle.
2. Divide these stitches evenly between 5 double-pointed needles (2 stitches per needle).
3. Using the 6th needle, commence knitting round 1.
4. On the next round * make 1, knit 2 *, repeat from * to * 5 times in all. You now have 15 stitches (3 stitches on each of five needles).
5. Knit the next round.

To commence the pentagon shape:

Round 1: * make 1, knit 2, make 1, knit 1, *. Repeat from * to * 5 times in all (25 stitches).
Rounds 2 and 3: knit.
Round 4: * make 1, knit 4, make 1, knit 1, *. Repeat from * to * 5 times in all (35 stitches).
Round 5: knit.

Continue in this manner, repeating rounds 1 to 4 above, but increasing the stitches by a factor of 2 on the increase round – for example * make 1, knit 2 (or 4, 6, 8), make 1, knit 1 *.

Round 3 is included to keep the knitting flat. You might find with thicker yarns that you can omit this extra round altogether, or include it only on every other repeat of the pattern. Experiment with yarns, needle size and stitch pattern. Stocking stitch will knit up to a different tension to garter stitch, for example.

below

Hexagon knitted on four double-pointed needles.

Hexagon

A six-sided geometric shape knitted on 4 double-pointed needles.

Method:

To knit from the centre to the outside edge, cast on 12 stitches on one double-pointed needle. Divide these stitches evenly between 3 double-pointed needles (4 stitches per needle). Each needle holds the stitches for two sides of the hexagon.

Round 1: using the 4th needle, commence knitting round one: * make 1 (yarn forward method), knit 1 *, repeat from * to * 12 times (24 stitches.
Rounds 2 and 3: knit both rounds.

Round 4: * make 1, knit 3, make 1, knit 1 *, repeat from * to * 6 times (36 stitches).

Round 5: knit.

Round 6: purl.

Round 7: * make 1, knit 5, make 1, knit 1 *, repeat from * to * 6 times (48 stitches).

Round 8 and 9: knit both rounds.

below

Knitted from the outer edges to the centre.

Note that there are 2 rounds knitted between each increase row. As with the previous example, the stitches are increased by a factor of 2 for each segment of the hexagon, for example * make 1, knit 5 (7, 9, 11), make 1, knit 1 *.

To knit **invisible increases**, the first increase round would read '* knit into the front and the back of the next stitch, repeat from * to * 12 times in all (24 stitches)'.

There are two segments on each needle, although you could, of course, knit the hexagon on 6 double-pointed needles with one spare working needle.

The samples on the previous page are examples of a square, rectangle and hexagon knitted on double-pointed needles expanding from the centre to the outside edge. Alternatively you can opt to commence knitting from the outside towards the centre.

The sample below shows an experimental swatch that commenced on four needles evenly divided as 20/20/20/20 stitches, and decreased down to 4/4/4/4. To create the funnel shapes in the centre of the swatches, continue knitting on these stitches for several rounds without altering the number of working stitches. Cast off when the required height is reached.

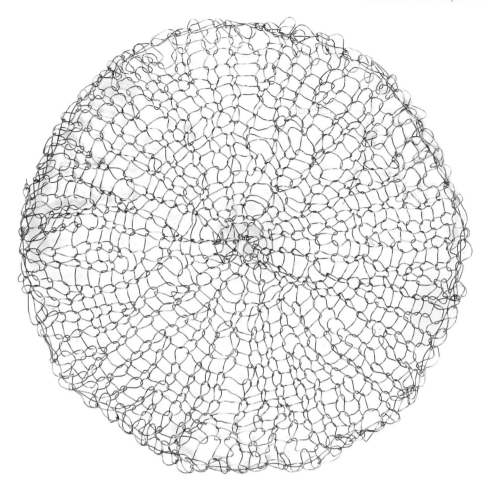

The sample above shows a circular shape. To knit a disc or circular shape such as this in stocking stitch, cast on 8 stitches on a double-pointed needle and knit 1 row. Divide the stitches evenly between four needles, and knit one round.

1. On the next round, increase once into every stitch; you now have 16 stitches.
2. Knit 3 rounds.
3. On the next round, increase once into every stitch; you now have 32 stitches.
4. Knit a further 3 rounds.
5. Increase once into every alternate stitch; you now have 48 stitches.
6. Knit a further 3 rounds.
7. Increase once into every 3rd stitch; you now have 64 stitches.
8. Knit 3 rounds.

Continue in this manner, increasing once into every 4th, 5th, 6th stitch etc. on each subsequent increase round, and at the same time continuing to knit 3 rounds between each increase round.

As always, the chosen yarn size, stitch patterns and needle sizes should be tested in the round before commencing a finished piece. In the example given there are always four increases (16 new stitches), evenly spaced on each of the four needles on every increase round. You might need to alter the number of rounds in between these rows if you find that the disc is curling up or becoming frilled around the edges – unless of course you want this to happen.

above

Circle knitted in 0.315 enamelled copper wire from the centre to the outside edges.

Three-Dimensional Forms

Three-dimensional forms have height, width and depth: for example, cones, cylinders, spheres and cubes. The samples below show the relationship between a two-dimensional square and a three-dimensional form that commenced on a square base.

Your choice of knitting medium, stitch structures and tension, and the relationship between these, will also determine the final shape of the form. For example, ribbing will draw the form inwards whereas garter stitch will knit up wider by comparison. Wire, gimp, strips of plastic and ribbon knit up into firm structures compared with softer yarns such as silk.

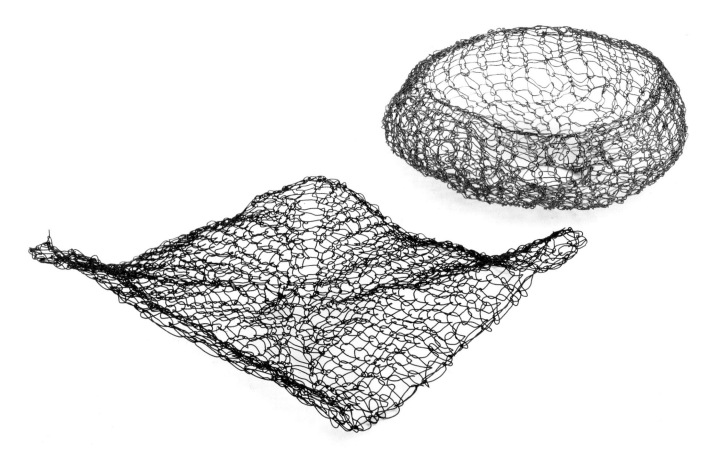

Cones and Cylinders

Open-ended tubes and cylinders are knitted in rounds, each subsequent round having the same number of stitches as the previous round for a regular shape. For a closed form with a base, start with a circular (or hexagonal) shape, as described above.

Multiple decreasing or increasing will create a cone shape (as in hats – knit top down or bottom up – or yoke sweaters). The idea here is to alter the total number of stitches on the needles evenly over one round. For example, 48 stitches decreased to 36 stitches means that you will need to decrease by 12 stitches in the next round thus: * knit 2 stitches, knit 2 together *, repeat from * to * to the end of the round.

above

Two- and three-dimensional related shapes and forms.

Forms on a Square Base

Forms that start from a square base invariably take on a more rounded appearance as they progress, due to the inherent elasticity in knitting. The extent to which this happens will, of course, depend on your chosen knitting medium.

Knitted in Gunmetal enamelled copper wire on 3.75mm (US size 5) needles, the square base of the sample opposite was extended outwards until there were 12 stitches on each of 4 needles. Next, straight sides were knitted on these 48 stitches in rounds of knit- and purl-facing stitches. Towards the top of the form there were regularly spaced decreases all the way around to draw the edges inwards.

The samples below show square and hexagonal basket bases. The sample on the left develops the square base, as described above, into a firm yet flexible basket. Expanded to 72 stitches and transferred to a circular knitting needle – 3mm (US size 2½), 40cm (16in) long, the first row is worked with 18 stitches in each of four colours.

The sample below right is knitted in gimp. It commences with a hexagonal base, which is expanded from 12 to 84 stitches as described above and knitted on 3.5mm (US size 4) double-pointed needles and changing to 3.00mm (US size 2½), 50cm (20in) length, circular needles at the point where the sides commence. About two thirds of the way up the basket, a round of multiple decreases was made thus: * knit 2 stitches, knit 2 stitches together *, repeat from * to * to the end of the round. Change to shorter length needles if necessary.

The small-size Premium circular knitting needles from Addi are ideal for this type of work, the shortest length of connecting cable being 30cm (12in) moving upwards in increments of 10cm (4in). Transfer stitches from the longer needles to a shorter length once it is not possible to connect the circle of stitches.

below

Free-standing vessels developed from a square and hexagonal base.

Forms on a Pentagon Base

The sample below is knitted on 6mm (US size 10) double-pointed needles in Texere gimp and recycled telephone wire. The base is increased outwards, as described above, until there are 11 stitches on each of five needles. The sides are knitted straight for several rows with an occasional purl row to vary the texture.

At regular intervals, multiple decreases are worked, starting from 55 stitches:

1. Knit 4, knit 3 together, knit 4 *. Repeat this instruction from * to * for each of the 5 needles (45 stitches).

2. On the next decrease row * knit 3, knit 3 together, knit 3 *. Repeat this instruction from * to * for each of the 5 needles (35 stitches).

3. On the next decrease row * knit 2, knit 3 together, knit 2 *. Repeat this instruction from * to * for each of the 5 needles (25 stitches).

4. Increase outwards as for the pentagonal base until you have 55 stitches and cast off.

below

Free-standing vessel
knitted in gimp and
recycled telephone cable.

Branching Forms

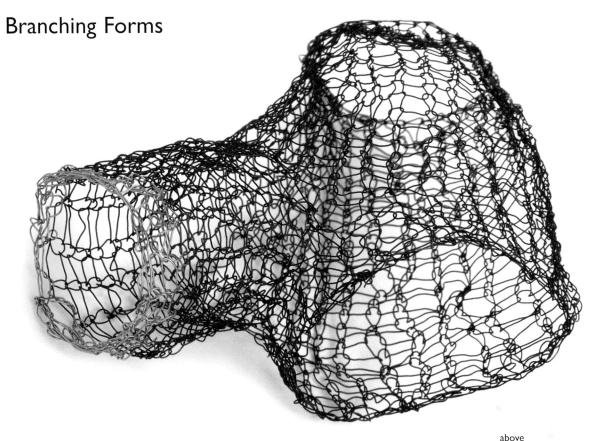

To make branching forms like these, study how the fingers and thumbs are constructed on gloves, where extra stitches are added on to accommodate the girth of individual fingers. Commence knitting a straight tubular form on double-pointed needles with 10 stitches cast on for each of four needles, knitting with a 5th needle. The idea is to create a wedge shape (to act as a gusset) at the beginning of one of these needles, by increasing stitches as you if you were knitting a thumb in the round.

Increase 1 stitch into the 1st stitch of the round by knitting into the front and back of it, knit 2 more stitches, increase 1 stitch into the next stitch and knit the remaining 6 stitches on this needle. You should now have 10 plus 2 new stitches on this needle. Knit the remaining 30 stitches from the next three needles without shaping (42 stitches). Knit three rounds.

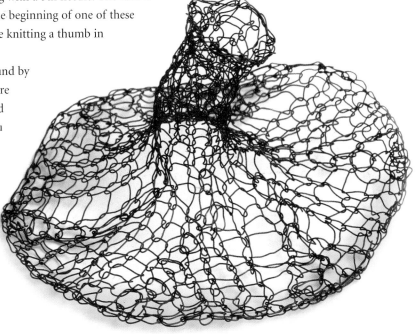

right

Funnel shape knitted using

a spiral-shaping technique.

Written in knitters' jargon the four rows would read:

Round 1: Kfb, K2, Kfb, K36 (42 stitches)
Rounds 2, 3 and 4: K

To continue the branch shape work as follows:

Round 5: Kfb, K4, Kfb, K36 (44 stitches)
Rounds 6, 7 and 8: K
Round 9: Kfb, K6, Kfb, K36 (46 stitches)
Rounds 10, 11 and 12: K
Round 13: Kfb, K8, Kfb, K36 (48 stitches)
Rounds 14, 15 and 16: K

The 18 stitches on the leading needle now need to be rearranged: divide the 8 new stitches between three short, double-pointed needles. Transfer the remaining 40 stitches onto stitch holders so they don't slip off.

right

Complex branching form.

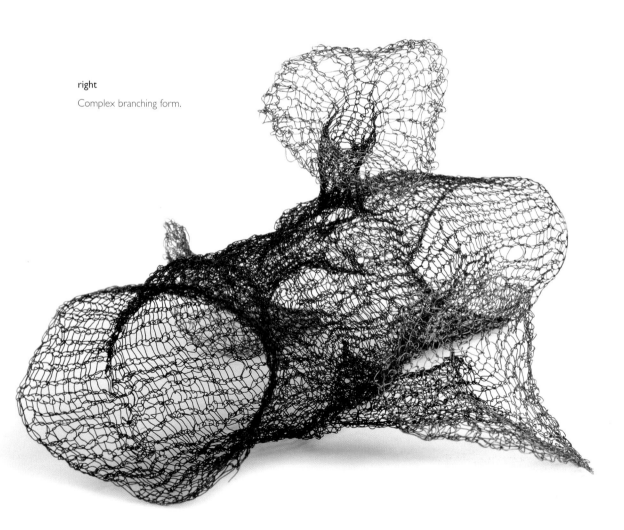

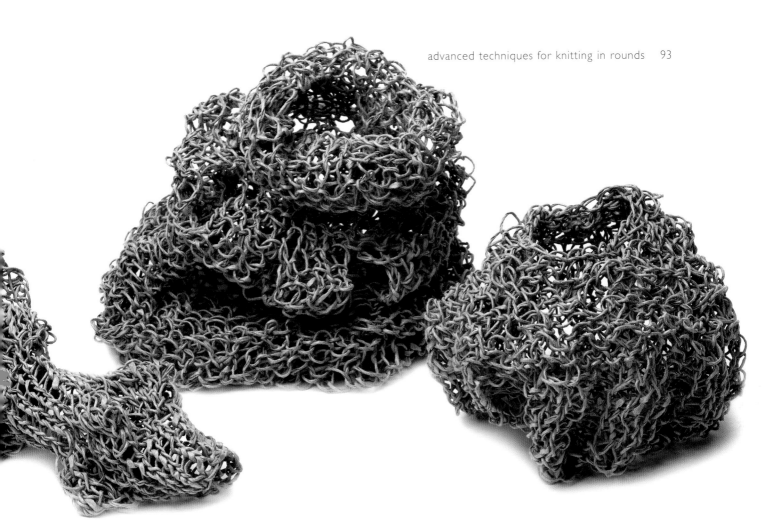

Knit the 8 new stitches, and cast on a further 4 stitches on another double-pointed needle to make a small-diameter round for the branch (thumb) – 2/3/3/4 stitches on each of 4 needles. Knit straight, in rounds, for the required depth and then cast off. (You can, of course, increase the number of stitches radically to make funnel shapes – as shown opposite – for example make 2 stitches from every alternate stitch.)

Return the 40 stitches from the stitch holders onto 4 double-pointed needles, along with 4 stitches from the cast-on stitches at the base of the branch, making a total of 44 stitches. Working in this manner means that the main tube (trunk) will gradually increase in girth every time you knit a new branch. Alternatively, decrease 4 stitches evenly spaced on the next round, making a total of 40 stitches.

The example opposite shows a complex branching form developed from previous samples knitted on 3.5mm (US size 4) double pointed needles.

above

Standing forms in paper cord.

Standing Forms in Paper Cord

The samples above show standing forms, a group of three-dimensional forms based on old gnarled tree trunks and cellular shapes. I knitted these directly from primary source material as if making drawings with yarn and needles. Knitted in strong paper cord, these pieces are designed to look organic and able to blend into a natural space. Made in multiples they might be developed into a grotto-like installation.

8 Pattern on Pattern

Stripe patterns derived from a single pair of Georgian shoes and altered texts are the two inspirations for this chapter. The first group of samples explores the relationship between surface pattern, shape and form, working with simple stripe patterns and a variety of shaping techniques, initially as single modules. These small self-contained pattern units can be repeated over and over again, used as single images or as the basis of three-dimensional form.

Continuing the stripe theme, reverse appliqué (Mola work) is explored as a way to create relief surfaces using pre-felted knitting. Wet felting basics are outlined below while the needle-felting techniques covered in chapter 9, show how you can further embellish the surface of the cut and stitched felts explained here.

The sample opposite is an example of a version of the striped shoe constructed for *Made from Memory*, an exhibition by the author inspired by the various items in the collection of Pickford's House Museum of Georgian Costume, Derby, UK. The example here was constructed from varnished, stitched and distressed Tyvek and held together with a fine web of metallic knitting that was also distressed and worked into.

Integrating Pattern, Shape and Form

These samples explore the relationship between surface pattern and the shaping process, the latter dictating the direction of the stripe patterns. In addition, see the group of geometric shapes knitted in the round in spiralling stripe patterns, in chapter 7 (pages 84–85).

The samples on the following pages show units of pattern exploring shaping techniques knitted in simple stripe patterns.

Regular, symmetrical increasing and decreasing is used to create the chevron pattern in the sample on page 96. With every decrease there is an equivalent increase in the same row, meaning that the number of stitches remains constant. The increases and decreases do not need to be adjacent to one another in the row. In this example, the decreasing takes place either side of a centre stitch, and the increasing takes place on the second stitch in from the left and right edges.

Most methods of increasing and decreasing result in a visible slant, with the stitches pointing either to the left or the right. To make a symmetrical stitch pattern, use paired decreases with a left and a right slanting combination of stitches.

In the sample below there is a left-slanting decrease worked as follows: before the centre stitch, slip two stitches knit-wise onto the right-hand needle, insert the left-hand needle into the front of both these stitches, from the left, and knit them off together. The two stitches immediately to the left of the centre stitch are knitted together by inserting the right needle into the front of both these stitches from left to right, and knitting them off together, creating a right-slanting decrease. The abbreviations for these decreases are SSK and K2tog.

To compensate for these two decreases, make a new stitch at the beginning and end of the same row using paired increases. One suitable working method is to purl then knit into the second stitch of the row, and knit then purl into the second to last stitch of the row.

Knitting a Chevron-Shaped Unit

The sample below was knitted in chiffon ribbon and Amaizing 100 per cent Corn Fibre from SWTC on 4mm (US size 6) bamboo needles.

Cast on an odd number of stitches – for example, 21 – then proceed as follows:

Row 1: knit 1 stitch, purl then knit into the next stitch (create 1 extra stitch), knit 6 stitches and make a left slanting decrease, SSK (decrease 1 stitch). Continue this row as follows: knit 1 (this is the centre stitch), make a right slanting decrease, K2tog (1 less stitch), knit 6 stitches, knit and purl into the next stitch (1 extra stitch), knit 1 stitch.

Row 2: knit or purl the next row without any further shaping.

Repeat these two rows as required, working exchanging colours A and B as determined by your pattern.

To knit a mirror image of this chevron, change the central decreases into increases and the decreases on the left and right edges into decreases.

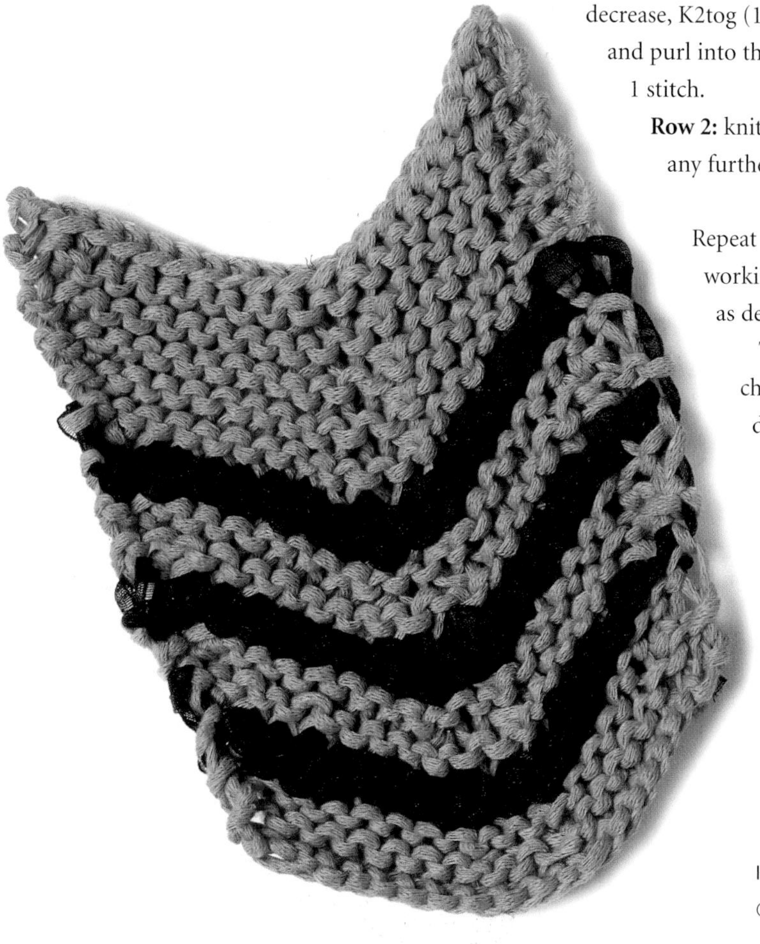

left

Chevron-shaped unit.

Sideways-Knitted Shaped Edgings

These samples are examples of pattern units that are knitted sideways. They can be broken down into a straight border followed by an increase (discreet or obvious), and finally a shaped-edge section. The number of increases on any given row will dictate both the length and angle of the shaped section. In the following example, one stitch is increased after the straight border section on every other row. Once you have reached the required number of stitches (the length of the pointed section) cast off until the original number of stitches remains.

The sample shown above right, the shaped section will be twice the width of that shown opposite, and becomes more oval in shape. The oval shape would be useful for the base of a vessel, where the edge loops can be picked up on double-pointed needles to knit the walls of the form.

To knit a similar swatch, cast on 6 stitches on 4mm (US size 6) needles in Amaizing (SWTC) Colour A and proceed as follows:

above

Oval-shaped unit.

1. Knit 2 rows.
2. Change to Colour B. Knit 4 stitches. Make 1 new stitch by purling and knitting into the next stitch, knit1. You should have 7 stitches on the needle. Knit back on these 7 stitches.
3. Change to Colour A. Knit 4 stitches. Make 1 new stitch by purling and knitting into the next stitch. Knit 2 stitches. You should have 8 stitches on the needle. Knit back on these 8 stitches.
4. Continue knitting in this manner increasing on alternate rows until there are 18 stitches on the needle.
5. Now start to shape the sample inwards, decreasing 1 stitch every alternate row until 6 stitches remain.

below

Triangular-shaped unit.

To knit the discreet increases in the sample shown right make a lifted increase thus:

Knit into the head of the stitch in the row below and then knit the stitch loop on the needles off. The SSK decrease (as described above) is used to narrow the shape, and is a made on the two stitches immediately after the four border stitches.

See also the beaded neckpieces and collars illustrated on pages 48–51, which were knitted in much the same way as the samples outlined above.

Striped Wedges in Short-Row Knitting

The sample shown right uses the same short-row knitting technique described in chapter 4, now knitted in many colours.

Assuming you have cast on (for example) 21 stitches and the aim is to knit a smooth wedge shape, you will need to add or subtract at least 1 extra stitch on every alternate row. For example, working in stocking stitch: knit 1, turn and purl back, knit 3 turn and purl back, and so on until you have knitted all stitches in this way.

To make a shallower wedge on the same number of stitches, knit more of the stitches in each row. For example, knit 7 turn and purl back, knit 14 turn and purl back 14, knit 21 turn and purl back 21.

If you want to knit wedges on the opposite side of the knitting, you will need to knit 1 extra row before commencing the wedge. If you are working in stocking stitch, the wedge will begin on a purl row and end on a knit row.

The sample below is knitted in the round on 3 needles over 33 stitches all rounds knit using the same method of shaping as the sample above. In circular knitting this is the same as knitting 1 row knit, 1 row purl on two needles, resulting in stocking stitch rather than garter stitch.

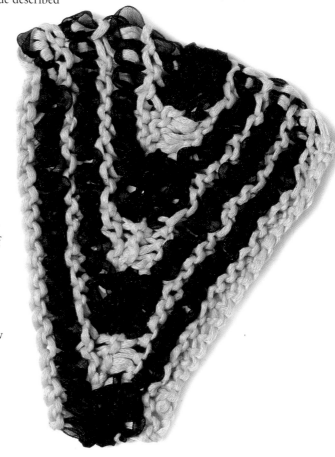

above

A wedge worked in a striking striped colour combination.

left

Pattern-knitting in the round.

Knit, Wrap and Turn

Note that at the point where you are turning the knitting in the examples above there is a visible eyelet. This can be used for decorative purposes, but you can also eliminate it by using one of the following three methods:

A) Wrapping the next stitch before turning the work.

B) Yarn over method.

C) Catching the loop from the row below, sometimes referred to as the preferred working method of Japanese knitters.

Method A

Knit or purl to the point where you want to turn the work. Slip the next stitch purl-wise to the right-hand needle. This simply means insert the right-hand needle from right to the left from the front into the next stitch on the left-hand needle, and transfer it to the right-hand needle. Bring the yarn forward between the needles and return the slipped stitch to the left-hand needle. Turn the work, either leaving the yarn at the back for a knit stitch or bringing it forward for a purl stitch. Knit or purl the next row.

To disguise the wraps, knit the tie in with the stitch it wraps, doing this on the first long row after the short row sections.

above
Repeat pattern.

below
Left- and right-facing wedges.

Working in Multiples

The sample above right is a development of the single pattern unit shown on page 97, and shows the effectiveness of repeating simple pattern units in multiples, so creating more complex shaped and patterned surfaces. It is knitted sideways on 6mm (US size 10) wooden needles in two colours of banana silk yarn (colours A and B), available from www.frabjousfibers.com.

This sample (right) illustrates sideways-knitted short-row wedges, where the broad edge faces to the right and then to the left, creating a meandering curved shape. To achieve this effect, knit an extra row, so that the new wedge commences from the opposite side of the knitting to the previous wedge.

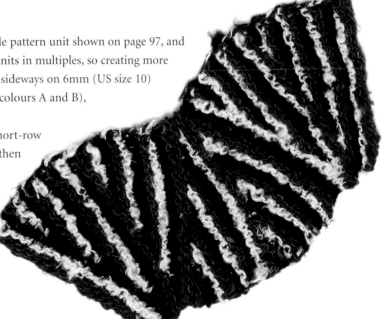

If you want a clearly defined stripe pattern, make the first wedge all rows knit and second wedge all rows purl. If you examine the front and back of a 2-row knit stitch in an 'all rows knit' strip pattern, you will see that one side is more textured and less defined than the other. These samples (below and detail, opposite) show strong tonal contrasts knitted in elastic, millinery material, gimp, and ribbon.

right
Detail of non-traditional samples shown below.

below
Short row knitting in non-traditional materials.

Felting Knitted Textiles

I describe the basics of felting knitting below, but please note that there are many specialist publications that can provide a more in-depth discussion of this subject.

Felt made from scratch involves stacking layers of unspun fibres in the shape of the finished piece, and subjecting them to beating and rolling, using hot water and soap, to compact the fibres into a dense fabric. Wool has a natural tendency to cling together when subjected to heat, moisture and friction, owing to the scaly surface of the wool fibre. To felt knitting, apply the same principles as for general felting, either processing the swatch by hand or in the washing machine.

Suitable Yarns

Choose wool fibres that will felt readily, for example 100 per cent pure wool such as Rowan four-ply Scottish tweed, 100 per cent Shetland wool from Jamieson and Smith or machine-knit weight merino and botany wool. (Remember that fine yarns intended machine knitting can always be bulked up for hand knitting.)

Check that the wool will actually felt before purchasing any great quantity of industrial oddment yarns. Often these yarns are machine washable, meaning that they have a special coating applied to smooth the surface of the wool fibre, intentionally inhibiting the felting process. Similarly, tightly twisted woollen carpet yarn is made to resist wear, and will only felt with great difficulty.

Gauge and Tension

Use a larger needle size than normal for any given yarn when knitting for felting. Larger stitches felt down more quickly than closely packed ones because the extra space allows more movement and friction, both of which speed up the felting process. Similarly, a two-colour stranded knitting pattern often felts down more quickly than a single colour fabric as the floats (the looped yarn) on the reverse of the knitting create extra friction.

Make two sample swatches, knitted in the same yarn and needle size. Felt one, and leave the other one untreated, so that you can compare the amount of shrinkage. The speed with which the felting process begins varies from fibre to fibre. For example, a very soft lambswool will felt so quickly that you really do need to watch it carefully if the finished size is important, in particular if you felt in the washing machine.

It is a good idea to compile a reference file of felted and untreated swatches. For example, make notes on the method of felting used (by hand or in the washing machine), the water temperature and the amount of time taken for the felting process to commence.

Technique

Before you start, take precautions to eliminate any allergic reaction that may occur when handling wet wool, fibres, fabric dye or detergents. I use a barrier cream and wear rubber gloves wherever possible. You might also consider using a face mask to avoid inhaling dust fibres during the felting process.

For hand felting you will need
access to both hot and cold water, a clear
work surface, heat-resistant rubber gloves, a
rough surface to felt onto (such as a small bamboo
blind), pure soap and a thermometer to test the
temperature of the hot water.

above

Felted and cut knitting.

First, soak the swatch to be felted in a bowl of lukewarm water
for approximately 30 minutes, to allow the fibres to swell and the surface
to open up. (If you are using oiled yarn, wash the swatch first in soapy water to remove the oil.)

Work between hot water and ice-cold water, making sure that the hot water is as hot as you
can bear without risk of scalding. Pure soap (never a harsh detergent) can be added to the hot
water to lubricate the yarn and thus speed up the felting process. However, it is not necessary for
fine soft yarns such as Merino.

Plunge the wetted-out swatch into the hot water, and then rub it vigorously between the
palms of your hands, or against the rough surface if practical to do so. Make sure you do this to
the whole of the swatch. The outer fibres of the wool will be starting to tangle and mesh
together. Next, plunge the swatch into the cold water to lock the fibres together.

Repeat this hot/cold process as many times as needed. You will notice a change in the handle
and density of the knitting as the felting proceeds. Felting cannot be reversed, but it can be
stopped at any point and then worked on further at a later time.

Cut and Layered Knitted Felts

Examples of cut, patterned fabrics can also be found in Mola work, a technique practised by the
Cuna Indians, using several layers of brightly coloured fabrics. These layers are cut through,
layer after layer, to reveal abstract and geometric patterns. The sample above shows a simple
stripe pattern in felting (wool) and non-felting (metallic) fibres. It was made by cutting into the
felted sections once they had been processed. Make similar swatches to practice cutting felted
knitting and to see how feltable and non-feltable yarns combine.

Layer (for example) three felts one on top of the other in a sandwich, facing the right side
uppermost, using a mix of plain, striped and patterned pieces. The top layers in the examples on
the following page are a shoe image. Pin and tack all the layers of the design together before
starting to machine stitch them. Tack large-scale work across the fabric, both horizontally and
vertically. Practice stitching through scrap layers of felts to find a suitable tension for straight
and satin stitches.

Using a straight stitch, sew around the outline of the pattern - in this instance the shoe design. Carefully cut through the *top layer* only, using a sharp pair of embroidery scissors to reveal areas of the next layer down. Machine stitch patterns on this layer, and cut through this second layer of felt to reveal some of the base layer.

To seal the cut edges, use hand-tooled needle felting (see chapter 9) or satin stitch machine stitching, or carefully wet-felt the whole piece again. The latter option will mean that the finished piece will shrink down further; this can be problematic if you are using combinations of felted materials that shrink at different rates, so always experiment first before embarking on a full-scale piece.

The samples shown here are examples of cut felts based on the Mola technique. The cut patterns in these examples have been machine stitched – to do the same you will need access to a sewing machine with a swing needle, and a really sharp pair of embroidery scissors. In the sample below, a more experimental sampling, I used a double layer of patterned knitted felts cut through to reveal the striped background. It was partially embellished with a needle-punch machine (see below) on the shoe image. The samples shown right are a development of this idea, each comprising three layers of plain and patterned felts, while the sample opposite shows felts applied to a screen-printed background, combining altered text and cut and varnished shoe images.

above

Cut felts embellished with a needle-punch machine.

left

Experimental sampling.

Pattern Graphs

Simple two-colour geometric patterns can be drawn directly onto knitters' graph paper using a
code for each of the colours, such as black and white squares or symbols such as O and X. Each
small rectangle on the graph paper represents one stitch.

 Proportional graph paper (in the ratio 4:3, for example – see below) allows for the fact that a
knit stitch is not square, and so ensures that a design drawn on the graph paper knits up to the
correct proportions. For example, a circle will remain a circle, rather than knitting up as an
ellipse, as would happen if a circle were drawn onto normal square-grid graph paper. As a rule,
square stitches are a rarity, although it is important to note that other variations might occur in
the height and width of stitches, dependent upon the type of stitch pattern being knitted and
your choice of knitting medium and tension.

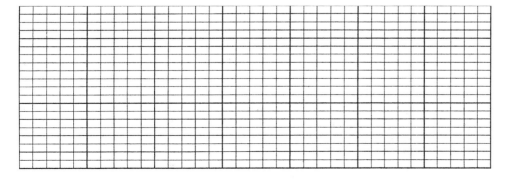

left

Knitter's graph paper has
rectangles rather than
squares, proportional to a
knitted stitch.

Translating Photos and Images to Graphs

To make a direct translation from drawings and photos into graph format you will need access to a computer, scanner, graphics software and a computer program such as Stitchpainter from Cochenille (see Suppliers, page 124). A full-colour import module is available to Stitchpainter Gold users, and allows you to import paintings and drawings from other computer graphics program directly into Stitchpainter, so that they can be turned into multicoloured knitting grids. However, remember that the same image spread over a small number of squares will result in a coarser, low-resolution version of the design than the same image over a larger number.

The graphs (shown right) were developed using Cochenille Stitchpainter, and were based on the artworks (shown below), which were scanned into a computer.

Knitting from Pattern Graphs

When working from a pattern graph, read the graph from the bottom to top. When knitting on two needles the graph is read from right to left for right-side rows and from left to right for wrong-side rows. For circular knitting, read the graph from right to left throughout.

The shoe images are translated into graph format and are intended for two-colour stranded knitting in 1 row knit, 1 row purl (or all rounds knit, for circular knitting). In this technique, knit (or purl) all the black squares in colour A, and all the white squares in colour B (or vice versa), stranding the colour not in use across the wrong side of the work.

Remember that a graph is simply a diagram; it does not form an exact equivalent of the actual size of a piece of knitting. Knitting two examples with the same number of rows and stitches from the same graph, one in handmade cordage on very thick needles and the other in lambswool on fine needles, will give finished pieces that are dramatically different in scale. It is essential to knit a tension swatch in your chosen knitting medium to establish the correct number of stitches and rows for any given size.

As a test, select areas from large graphs and knit a series of experiments in a range of knitting media and needle sizes. You will be able to compare the results and consider how best to use them in more resolved sampling, and then in finished products and artefacts.

below

Artworks prepared for scanning.

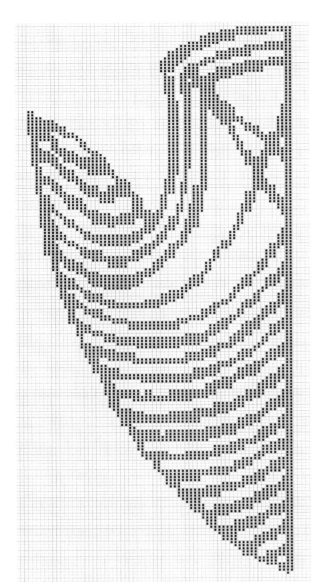

left

Refined shoe graph
created in Stitchpainter.

below

Simplified shoe graph.

bottom

Refined shoe graph.

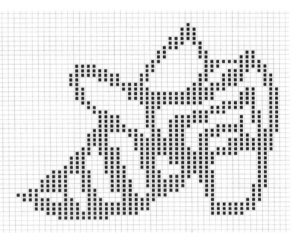

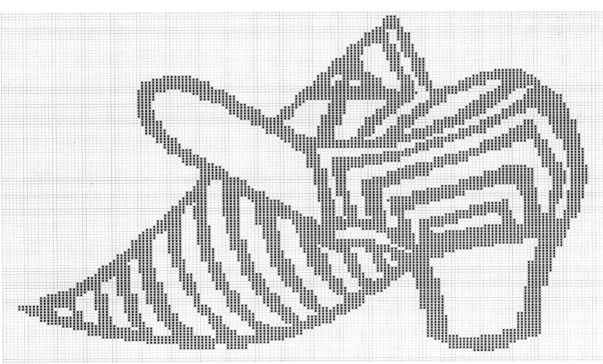

9 Decorative Surface Treatments

One short chapter cannot do justice to the many possible ways of embellishing and manipulating the surface of knitting. So I shall provide a brief introduction to just what can be achieved, and refer you to books on surface decoration for additional inspiration – for example on bringing dyeing, printing and stitching into knitting.

Included in this chapter are simple off-loom techniques, generally associated with basketry and ceremonial artefacts in ancient cultures, such as wrapping and binding. These are worked in conjunction with slitted knitted fabrics that were created through short-row knitting and buttonhole techniques. Buttons and copper embellishments complement these pieces. Needle felting, colouring, stiffening and methods of distressing knitted surfaces are also touched on briefly.

Wrapping and Binding Techniques

Wrapping and binding fibres around themselves, or with another yarn, is a simple yet effective technique. Wrapping endows otherwise fragile or flexible fibres with rigidity and strength, and also provides a way of holding groups of fibres together for functional or decorative purposes.

For wrapping, the only tools you might need are a tapestry needle and scissors. Lengths of yarn are wrapped around a core of fibres or around columns of knitting. The bindings should be done tightly and at regular intervals. Tail ends need to be secured at the beginning and end of the wrapped section.

right

Copper embellishments enhance the texture and colour of this piece as well as providing a change of pace.

Securing the Ends

There are several methods for securing the tails of
the wrapping yarn. When choosing one, consider such
factors as the relative strength of the wrapping yarn, the
length of the wrapped section, and also
the types of yarns and fibres being used
for the core and the bindings.

The simplest method is to lay the tail
of the wrapping yarn parallel to the core
from, say, left to right, and then start wrapping
back over the core and the tail of yarn from right to left. To secure the other end, you can make
a loop with the remaining part of the tail, and lay this parallel to the core. Continue to wrap
around the core and the extra tails of yarn towards the loop. Insert the wrapping yarn through
the loop. Pull taut so the wrapping yarn travels down through the bindings. Cut off the tail ends.

The second method is to use a large-eyed tapestry needle to pull the wrapping yarn through
the bindings. This method works best with short sections of wrapping, and where the wrapping
yarn is thin enough to go through the eye of a tapestry needle. Thread up the needle and pull
the wrapping thread all the way through the complete length of the binding, tightening the coil,
if needed, by twisting the needle gently. Cut off the tail ends of yarn.

The third method works as follows: begin by laying the wrapping yarn from left to right,
parallel with a length of solid core, for example washing line. Now wrap back over the core from
right to the left over the core and the long tail end. Arrange the wrapping yarn at right angles to
the core before you start binding back towards the left. Wrap tightly and evenly.

At the midway point of the bindings, lay a loop of strong yarn over the remainder of the core
yarn. The loop should point to the left and the two loose ends point towards the right,
overlapping the area you have just wrapped. Continue binding the core and the loop as one.
When the wrapping is completed, use the loop from the auxiliary yarn to pull the tail end of the
wrapping yarn through the bindings to secure it. Insert the tail end of the wrapping yarn
through the loop while keeping your finger on the binding to stop it coming undone. Pull both
ends of the auxiliary yarn to the right to draw the wrapping yarn under the binding from left to
right. Cut off the loose tail ends.

The final method uses a U-shaped loop made in the actual wrapping yarn to draw the end
through the binding. You need to use a strong yarn to wrap with, or it will break when you pull
the end through. Lay the wrapping yarn parallel to the core in a U shape. Hold the core thread
in the left hand, and start wrapping with the right hand over the core and towards the U. Once
complete, insert the end of yarn you have been wrapping with through the U-shaped loop and
hold it tight. Pull the end of yarn protruding from the right-hand end of the wrapped section so
that the left end of the wrapping yarn is drawn up through the wrapped section to secure it
tightly. You will feel the end travelling up through the wrapping if you have done this correctly.

Suitable Knitted Surfaces

The samples here and on the following page show a range of knitted surfaces suitable for
wrapping and binding, including vertical and horizontal slitted surfaces bound in contrasting

above
Wrapped knitting using
the big buttonhole
technique to create
horizontal slits, decorated
with copper
embellishments.

opposite
Wrapped knitting, layered
over knitted felts.

fibres. The two main working methods explained below are horizontal slits, worked as you would a buttonhole but on a larger scale, and vertical slits, which are knitted in short row technique. Of course you can also wrap groups of threads and knitted cords, as shown on page 112 (bottom) for example.

Big Buttonholes

These samples (above left and right) show horizontal columns made using casting on and off techniques.

To knit a similar swatch to those shown, cast on 12 stitches and knit 4 rows (for example) and then work from the pattern sequence outlined below. Essentially you are knitting big buttonholes one above the other.

> **Row 1:** knit 3 stitches, cast off 6 stitches and knit the remaining 3 stitches.
> **Row 2:** knit 3 stitches, cast back on 6 stitches using two needles and knit the remaining 3 stitches.

Incidentally, a tip for making a two-needle cast-on in the middle of the row is to turn the knitting around as if you are about to work back to the end of the row. Cast on the stitches required and then turn the knitting back again to continue knitting to the end of the row. Ensure that the first and final stitch of the casting on are pulled tight against the existing stitches to avoid a gap on the next row.

Variations for the above example include knitting a greater number of rows before repeating rows 1 and 2 to make wider columns, or alternating wide and narrow bars of knitting, or simply repeating the two rows to create thin columns throughout. The idea is to bind the latter and leave the former unwrapped.

The sample above left shows horizontal slits, wrapped in Colinette Tao 100 per cent silk and decorated with handmade copper embellishments by Mick Pearce. It was knitted in a mix of recycled sari yarn (New Zealand Yarn Traders) and Colinette Firecracker on 4.5mm (US size 7) Brittany Birch needles.

The sample right was knitted in banana silk yarn (100 per cent rayon) on 5mm (US size 8) Brittany Birch needles, layered over patterned and felted Rowan Scottish tweed and decorated with vintage buttons.

Vertical Columns

These samples (right and below) use short-row knitting techniques (see chapter 4) to knit a series of linked, vertical columns in which each band of columns is divided by full-row knitting.

Cast on 20 stitches and knit several rows in a stitch pattern of your choosing. Subdivide the knitting into groups of, say, 5 stitches. Knit (for example) 10 rows back and forth on the first group, and break off the yarn. Transfer these 5 stitches to a stitch holder (Addi brand is long enough to hold several of these 'columns-in-waiting' until you are ready to work with them again). Move onto the next 5 stitches and do the same thing again. Once you have done the same for all stitches, transfer them from the holder back onto the main working needle.

You can vary the width and height of the columns, the amount of rows between each band of columns and, of course, the texture and colour of the materials you choose to work with. You could make each subsequent column gradually longer or shorter than the previous column, or even cross over the columns by transferring the groups of stitches back onto the working needle in the 'wrong' order, so interweaving the columns as you work.

above

Wrapped knitting using the short-row technique to create vertical slits, with vintage buttons.

below

Fabric, with vertical slits, in knit and purl patterns decorated with copper embellishments.

Needle Felting

The basics of the wet felting process were covered in chapter 8. Needle felting is a dry felt-making process that uses a barbed felting needle to tangle the wool fibres together. The process has been in operation since the beginning of the last century, initially as an industrial technique. Large beds of steel needles are moved in and out of the web of loose fibres, mechanically interlocking them, and the felts produced are sometimes referred to as needle-punched felts,

The same technology can be applied to knitted felts. In this process, you are essentially using barbed needles to laminate the surface fibres of the combed wool tops (or rovings) onto a base of felted knitting. Materials such as fine fabric (see samples, above) also bond well onto knitted felts, especially when using an embellishing machine (see below). Felting needles can be used on dry, carded wool tops or fleece, as well as synthetic fibres that are resistant to wet felting.

The embellishing machine's barbed needles pull the fibres downwards, locking and compressing them without the need of either soap or water. The lower section of the needle is triangular, with barbs cut into the edges. The barbs are cut facing one direction and the tangling process occurs when the needle is pointed downwards, not when it is pulled out. With each subsequent movement of the felting needles the mass of wool fibres moves, tangles and compresses down into a denser mass.

Equipment

The barbed needles for craft purposes are made from hardened steel, and can be used either individually or in a small cluster fitted into a wooden handle, or they can be mounted in a special head on a dedicated embellishing machine. Various types of needle punch machines, manufactured for the purpose of embellishing fabrics in the same way as a hand-held tool, are available on the market.

You will need a selection of felting needles, which are available in different sizes and for different purposes. In addition you will require a support surface to felt into, such as extruded polystyrene building insulation material (not expanded polystyrene, which crumbles), a foam pillow or a needle felting mat. The material should be hard and dense enough to support the fabric you are embellishing, while allowing the needles to travel through smoothly without blunting them, and it also acts as a buffer between your body and the work in progress.

A few words on safety – be careful, felting needles are very sharp and can cause serious injury if not used properly and carefully. Take particular care that you do not stab yourself with them, watching your fingers at all times. Always keep the felting equipment out of reach of children and pets. If you are working with a multi-headed tool, always keep it in its protective tube when not in use. Single felting needles can be stored safely with their points pushed into a polystyrene block, protecting both the needle and the needle owner.

Technique

Place the foam pillow or similar onto a firm working surface and place the pre-felted knitting on this. Lay a thin web of fibres, teased out from the coloured wool roving, in the desired shape, on top of the pre-felted knitting. Needle-felt the shape into place by moving the felting needle smoothly in and out, in a straight motion.

Start with deep jabs that go through into the knitted base, to ensure the base felt and the loose fibres are being tangled together. Continue to work into the fibres until they are holding firmly to the knitted base. Turn the piece at regular intervals, building up the layers gradually. The more the felting needle is pushed into the fibres, the tighter the felting becomes.

Shallow jabs of the felting needle will felt the outer layers, and deeper jabs felt into the lower layers. You can add more tops (rovings) at any time. Once you have build up a layer of fibres into the knitting, you can choose to felt more deeply into certain areas.

Angle the felting needles to build up relief patterns that add textural interest, but always withdraw the felting needle at the same angle it entered the fabric, since the fine felting needles are prone to breakage if twisted during use. Apply the felting needle to selected shapes only where you want deeper areas of relief modelling.

Painting with Yarns and Fibres

Painting with yarns and fibres might seem to be a contradiction in terms, but working with unspun tops onto solid coloured grounds is a very painterly process, not unlike working with strokes of broken colour in oil pastels or paint, or using coloured embroidery threads in stitched textiles. Needle felting allows you to build low-relief areas in the work, as you might make a collage, in which layers of pattern and textures are applied one on top of the other to create a kaleidoscope of images. The intensity of the bright base colours in the knitting can give depth and life to colours laid over them, with areas of knit left to show through. This will also provide texture, that differs depending upon whether you choose to use the knit or purl face of the stocking-stitch swatch.

The samples on page 113 are examples of needle felting made on an embellishing machine, combining pre-felted knitting (Jamieson and Smith Shetland wool and Rowan Scottish tweed) with very fine silk georgette and recycled Sari yarn.

Painting, Dyeing and Varnishing

You can alter the colour of paper yarn with acrylic inks or dyes, either before or after knitting with them.

The sample on page 51 (top) shows hand-painted and varnished paper yarn used in short-row knitting techniques, then coloured once the knitting was complete. It is sometimes difficult to ensure that the colouring medium (in this case acrylic inks) penetrates right through the layers of the knitting. Try painting the tape prior to knitting and then further embellishing the work once the piece has been knitted. The sample below shows hand-painted and varnished paper beads knitted in pre-coloured paper yarn and enamelled copper wire (Scientific Wire Company). The finished piece was given a coating of French polish – if you use this product, do refer to the safe handling instructions printed on the label.

To pre-colour short lengths of yarn, wind a length around a tall glass jar, securing the ends with duct tape. Paint directly onto the paper string, ensuring that the colouring medium has penetrated right through. Leave in a warm place to dry. For blended colours dampen the paper yarn before applying the colour, letting one colour bleed into the next for a rainbow dye effect.

You can also, of course, over-dye commercially produced yarns (see handmade yarn samples, page 33). Remember to follow the guidelines relating to the safe use of dye powder (wear a mask and gloves, and work in a well-ventilated area, for instance).

Waxing small amounts of paper yarn adds yet another finish to the surface. To do this, colour the paper string as outlined above (or use in its natural state), drying it out thoroughly before applying the wax coating. Draw the paper yarn across a candle to coat the surface with wax. Waxed paper string is much easier and stronger to manipulate, resulting in a pliable and robust knitting medium.

Use PVA glue to stiffen surfaces, in particular for paper knitting. You will need to mould the knitted piece over a rigid form – a wok covered in cling film is the ideal shape for a bowl form. Varnishes including French polish (shellac dissolved in alcohol) work well on felted knits as a stiffener, but do take note of any health and safety issues.

below

Detail from a handmade paper bead panel, knitted in wire and paper yarn.

More Ideas

The sample collection (shown right) shows small-scale experimental patches and finished artwork in a mix of media, including Tyvek in fabric and sheet form.

Tyvek is an interesting material to work with: not only can you colour it before or after knitting, but it is also receptive to further surface treatments, such as distressing with a hot-air tool or a small soldering iron. (See *Surfaces for Stitch*, by Gwen Hedley (Batsford), for more detailed instructions on working with plastics such as Tyvek.) As with other techniques, you need to be aware of any health and safety issues relating to fumes from burning plastic and other materials. If in any doubt about your personal safety and others working in close proximity, seek advice from a qualified source.

The photograph below is an image from my work *Relics*, a piece based on ideas concerned with protection. The work is made from distressed, coloured, varnished and knitted Tyvek fabric, knitted sideways-on using increases and cast-off rows to create the shape. (See chapter 8 for examples and a description of the knitting technique.) The beads were made from rolled Tyvek, wrapped in enamelled copper wire and distressed with a hot-air tool.

above

Felted and varnished knitting combined with perforated Tyvek.

left

Relics – knitted and distressed Tyvek, with handmade beads made from Tyvek and wire.

The sample below provides a further example of the many ways of embellishing and manipulating the knitted surface. This chapter can only provide a brief survey, and aesthetic decisions on how to incorporate these techniques into your work remain with you, the artist. Knitting simply becomes another way of making marks and textures, to be incorporated into multilayered surfaces.

Combined, the component parts and individual materials and techniques used in a piece of work form an integrated whole. The onlooker is, ideally, unaware of the separate elements on viewing the work as a piece of art or craft. Only close inspection may reveal the making process, for example a combination of knitted Tyvek or fine sewing thread, layered between block-printed images and distorted wire. For more examples of combined techniques, see the examples from my logbooks in the next chapter.

below

Painted and distressed Tyvek has been knitted then layered over printed and painted Tyvek.

10 Creative Journeys

In this final chapter, let me take you on a creative journey from inspiration to completion, through examples from my own work.

My personal interest in knit lies in a contemporary interpretation of an ancient craft using either modern materials or a new 'take' on traditional fibres. Of particular interest to me is how ideas evolve through the making process, and the symbiotic relationship between materials, working processes and concepts. I am fascinated by the transformation of simple, linear materials into complex structures and surfaces that appear to grow magically, through the repetition of a single knitted stitch or pattern unit, to create shape and form.

The linear aspect of knit as a metaphor for a journey and a way of marking time intrigues me. Interlinked stitches and rows can become broken over time (as with paper yarn or rattan), so disrupting the original pattern, yet creating something new. Knit is a metaphor for many of the underlying ideas behind my current fibre arts work; for example the cyclic nature of growth and decay. The act of knitting builds organically, one stitch at a time very much like cells multiply in the natural world. Unravel knit and you are left with a length of thread to start all over again.

I choose materials either to express ideas and concepts, or because they themselves suggest an idea to me by the way they handle, their tactile qualities or their potential as metaphor. As a working method, the quiet, meditative process of hand knitting allows me to listen to the spaces in between: rhythmic and repetitive, the stitches are often formed intuitively, allowing me time to reflect on the concepts behind current and future work, and on life in general. The process of developing ideas as I work really is like a journey. It can be open-ended or with a specific purpose or destination in mind.

Spirit Dresses

Spirit Dress 1 (right) was originally made in 2003 for *Inside Out*, an exhibition of indoor and outdoor fibre arts pieces, inspired by and reflecting the peace and tranquillity of the grounds of Norton Priory Museum in Cheshire, UK. *Spirit Dresses* 3 and 4 (see following page) were created for *Knit 2 Together – Concepts in Knitting* (UK Crafts Council exhibition, 2005).

right

Spirit Dress 1, knitted in single-core connecting wire.

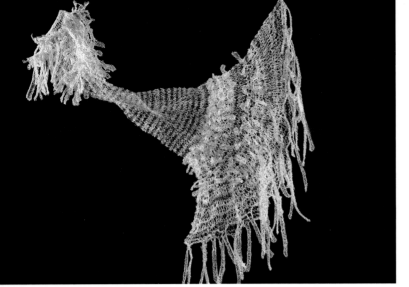

I chose single-core bell wire (connecting wire) as the knitting medium for *Spirit Dresses* 1 and 2. Weatherproof, and suited to hand knitting on huge circular needles, it had just enough rigidity to keep the shape of linear openwork stitch patterns. From a distance the work looked fragile and ghostly, the organic nature of the stitch structures working in harmony with the outdoor setting. This appearance was in direct contrast to the industrial nature of the manufactured connecting wire, creating skeletal structures devoid of an outside covering.

Spirit Dresses 3 and 4 (above) brought the 'outside' back inside, being designed for an indoor exhibition. These pieces combined wire and paper yarn to express ideas relating to permanence and fragility. I knitted the initial samples for these works in white wire and paper yarn, and explored ways of creating organic, linear patterns. I wanted to create harmonious works with an emphasis on structure and an absence of colour.

Pages from my logbook show work for *Spirit Dresses* 3 and 4 (see below). Many of the stitch patterns are worked out using the Fibonacci number system (see below), and aim to look and feel organic, as if inspired by natural forms. Old gnarled tree forms and branching shapes also supplied me with a source of inspiration.

The working method described below is simply an interesting starting point for beautifully proportioned pattern and textured knitting, and an exciting use of number systems. At the same time, this influences the relationship between the height and width of stitch sizes, different weight and thickness of yarns, and the balance between negative and positive patterns.

The Fibonacci sequence is named after Leonardo Pisano, a 13th-century Italian mathematician who also went under the name of Fibonacci. It consists of the infinite numerical series 1, 1, 2, 3, 5, 8 … in which, after the initial 1, each number is the sum of the two previous numbers. The ratios between adjacent numbers (for example 3 and 5, or 5 and 8) have often appealed to humanity's sense of beauty, and the series appears in art, architecture, music and poetry. These proportions are also found in the growth patterns of plants and animals (for instance, in the structure of pine cones or the grouping of seeds, flowers and petals). Ratios between larger consecutive Fibonacci numbers come very close to the Golden Section or Golden Ratio, an irrational number (one with an infinite number of decimal places) that is approximately 1.618 – this has often been regarded by artists as the 'perfect' aesthetic proportion.

above

Spirit Dresses 3 and 4, knitted in ivory enamelled copper wire and white paper yarn.

below

Pages from author's sketchbook.

White Shoes

Somewhere in one of my sketchbooks, I remember noting that my spirit dresses needed spirit shoes! Specifically, they needed ethereal, ghostly shoe-like forms to transport the spirit to another place. I used pure, simple unadorned shapes: the worldly, upper-class Georgian shoe, stripped of all its finery to express notions of spirituality.

White suggests innocence and purity in Western cultures. But in some Eastern cultures it is symbolic of death and mourning, and acknowledges the fact that the deceased has left the earth for a new, purer spiritual state. My shoes were made without soles, removing all notions of functionality – these shoes are not for wearing. They are incapable of holding weight, and do not need to, hence the use of light, delicate, fragile materials

Constructed from knitted sewing thread bonded to fine Tissutex papers, the white shoe installation relates directly to concepts explored in the making of *Spirit Dresses* 1 and 2. It is made in response to a single pair of upper-class women's shoes in the collection of Pickford's House Museum of Georgian Costume, Derby, for my exhibition *Made from Memory*.

The pieces below are examples of works from the same exhibition that explored the concept of protection, rediscovery and intrigue in seemingly ancient artefacts, through the medium of knitting and other textile techniques. For example *Relics* (below) and *Hand Me Downs* (below right) were inspired partly by a single pair of upper-class shoes in the museum collection, and also by concealed shoes found in many different types of buildings, having been placed there for traditional reasons.

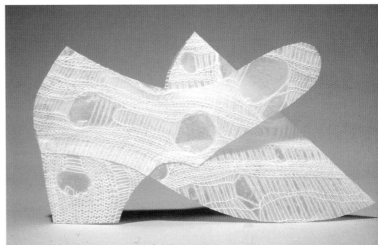

above

White shoe (above) and white shoe installation (top).

below

Relics shoe (left) and *Hand Me Downs* shoe (right).

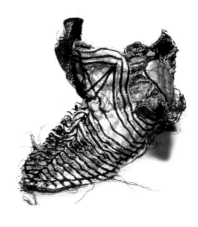

As a spin-off from this work, these pieces show examples of wire-knitted jewellery, developed as a direct result of *Made from Memory*, that reference the more decorative aspects of Georgian costume.

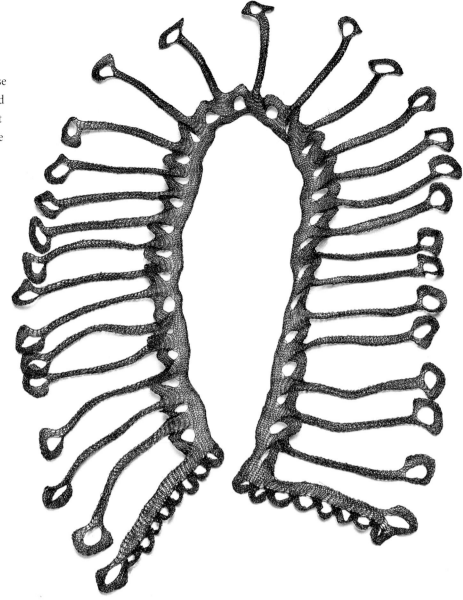

right

Frond boa.

below

Wire-knitted cuffs.

Knitting as Art

Familiarity with a variety of construction techniques, use of colour and treatments of knitting medium, good manipulative skills and sensitivity in the handling of materials and techniques – all are necessary practical skills for the serious contender in fibre arts practice. All these and more must be integrated with creative thinking, good studio practice, some maths, and an understanding of fibre technology.

Knitting as textile art demands an ability to make intelligent decisions as to the most suitable materials for translating initial ideas into something tangible, whether for installation work or for personal use. It is for the individual practitioner to decide which materials or techniques offer the best potential for a particular purpose or concept, and that is why filling sketchbooks with images and inspirational notes is a necessary adjunct to workshop practice.

Materials and fibres can be very seductive, and it is sometimes tempting to go for instant effects. But a more focused experimentation will yield more sophisticated results than the initial samples, where you might simply have been trying a fibre out for the first time. Remember that materials, as metaphors for ideas and concepts, engage the viewer on many different sensory levels. They invite a questioning approach to the work. For example, items traditionally knitted in wool in a particular technique might suggest a certain cosiness, homeliness and warmth, or they might evoke memories and links with another time or place. On the other hand, wool could be used to invoke a completely different response if the object appears soft and woolly but in reality somehow has sinister undertones, or deals with challenging issues. Alternatively, you could use materials in a covert way, as suggested in the conclusion to chapter 9: for instance, an expressive surface design might transform materials and techniques beyond recognition, to evoke a particular mood.

below

Pages from the author's sketchbook.

Consideration must be been given to the use of line, tone, shape, form, colour and texture, as well as to the principles of repetition, symmetry, balance, proportion and composition. Beautifully made, considered sampling underpins contemporary textile practice, while informing the next step in the development process.

To create surface patterns and textures in knitting that go beyond the obvious, hands-on experimentation will help you to express your concepts. Think with your hands and, above all, enjoy the challenge of creating unique works that not only stretch your own imagination, but extend the art of knitting into the 21st century.

Suppliers

Yarns

Colinette Yarns Ltd (UK)
Banwy Workshops
Llanfair
Caerinion
Powys,
Wales, SY21 0SG
Tel: 01938 810128
Fax: 01938 810127
Email: feedback@colinette.com
Web: www.colinette.com

Colinette Yarns Ltd (US)
Unique Kolours
28N. Bacton Hill Road
Malvern, PA 19355, USA
Web: www.uniquekolours.com

Texere Yarns Ltd
College Mill
Bakerend Rd
Bradford, BD1 4AU
Tel: 01274 722191
Fax: 01274 393500
Email: info@texereyarns.co.uk
Web: www.texereyarns.co.uk
(Large range of yarns including many suitable for dyeing.)

Rowan Yarns
Green Lane Mill
Holmfirth
West Yorkshire, HD9 2DX
Email: mail@knitrowan.com
Web: www.knitrowan.com
(Rowan Scottish tweed, suitable for felted knitting. Rowan yarn stockists directory can be viewed on their web-site.)

Jamieson & Smith (Shetland Wool Brokers) Ltd
90 North Road
Lerwick
Shetland Island, ZE1 0PQ
Scotland
Tel: 01595 693579
Fax: 01595 695009
Email: sales@shetlandwoolbrokers.co.uk
Web: www.shetland-wool-brokers.zetnet.co.uk
(100 per cent pure wool from the Shetland Islands, lace weight and jumper weight suitable for felted knitting.)

Yarn Traders
Helen Walker
3 Kent Street
Stoke
Nelson 7011
New Zealand
Email: helen@yarntraders.co.nz
Web: www.yarntraders.co.nz
(Suppliers of exotic natural yarns including banana silk and Kashmir sari ribbon.)

South West Trading Company Inc
Web: www.soysilk.com
See www.viridianyarns.com for UK stockists
(100 per cent soy silk and bamboo yarns.)

Frabjous Fibers
Email: stephanie@recycledsilk.com
Web: www.frabjousfibers.com
(Suppliers of banana silk, 100 per cent rayon, recycled silk, cotton, rayon and blends, natural fibres including hemp, nettle, aloo and charka cotton.)

Jan Hicks
Email: hicksangora@tiscali.co.uk
(100 per cent hand-dyed spun kid mohair).

Wire

Scientific Wire Company
18 Raven Road
South Woodford
London E18 1HW
Tel 020 8505 0002
Fax 020 8559 1114
Email: dan@wires.co.uk
Web: www.wires.co.uk

Knitting needles and accessories

Addi knitting needles
Web: www.addinadeln.de
(All types of knitting needles, needle gauges and stitch holders.)

Pony
For stockist information email:
info@thekingdoms.co.uk or call 0118 973 5196,
quoting 'Pony'.
(Products available nationwide from good fabric, craft and haberdashery stores.)

Brittany Birch
Artesano Ltd
28 Mansfield Rd
Reading
Berkshire RG1 6AJ
Tel 0118 9503350
Fax 0118 9503383
Email: knittingneedles@mcn.org
Web: www.brittanyneedles.com

Kollage Yarns
Email: info@KollageYarns.com
Web: www.KollageYarns.co
(Square knitting needles.)

Embellishments

Mick Pearce
Email: langdalepike@hotmail.com
(Handmade copper embellishments.)

G J Beads
Unit L, St Erth Industrial Estate
Rose-an-Grouse
Hayle
Cornwall TR27 6LP.
Tel: 01736 751 070
www.gjbeads.co.uk
Email: info@gjbeads.co.uk

Swiftbox
Tel: 01252 849571
Email: info@swiftbox.co.uk
Web: www.swiftbox.co.uk
(Suppliers of organza ribbons.)

Computer software

Cochenille Stitchpainter
Email: info@cochenille.com
Email UK: GillianLamb@netscape.net
Web: www.cochenille.com
(Available in standard and gold versions for Windows and Macintosh computers see website for worldwide distributors.)

Easy Knit
Fulford Software Solutions
Tel: 0115 9678761
Email: support@easycross.co.uk

Index